SpeedPro Series
How to build
TIGER AVON or GTA
SPORTS CARS FOR ROAD OR TRACK
33
88 TGR
UPDATED & REVISED NEW EDITION
Jim Dudley
Build YOUR own dream sports car on a small budget! • Based mainly on Ford Sierra mechanical components • Choose your own engine, including Ford Pinto OHC & Zetec or other 4-cylinder engines • Includes chassis drawings • GRP manufacturing & fabrication • Car assembly • Now includes conversion of an existing Avon to a GTA

Introduction & thanks

INTRODUCTION

It was when I was around twelve or thirteen years of age that the Lotus Seven came to have a great influence on me. I first caught sight of one whilst cycling near Dartford in Kent. The Lotus was parked, so I stopped and had a good look round it: the impression the car made was so great that there and then I promised myself I'd own one by the time I was twenty. As a boy I had no idea what I'd end up doing as a job, but I'm proud to say that I did achieve that boyhood ambition!

The author testing the new all-alloy RS6 race car.

I've owned and worked on many Lotus Sevens and I've raced (cars and karts) and rallycrossed too. I formed Tiger Racing in 1989 and, today, the company produces eight different models of Tiger Sports car, and is known worldwide for the Z100WR, which has been timed accelerating from 0-60mph in a staggering 2.8 seconds (at the time of writing, the quickest recorded time for a road legal sports car)!

This book majors on building a Tiger Avon sports car at low cost; however, the information it contains – which is based on years of practical experience – will give the reader valuable information on all aspects of

OTHER GREAT BOOKS FROM VELOCE

Important! All the technical drawings in this book are copyright and are intended to be used to produce a single Tiger Avon car. The drawings, photos and text are not to be photocopied, scanned or duplicated in any manner and are very strictly for private use. Any use of information from this book for commercial purposes or unlicensed dissemination will lead to prosecution.

Speedpro Series

4-Cylinder Engine Short Block High-Performance Manual – New Updated & Revised Edition (Hammill)
Alfa Romeo DOHC High-performance Manual (Kartalamakis)
Alfa Romeo V6 Engine High-performance Manual (Kartalamakis)
BMC 998cc A-series Engine, How to Power Tune (Hammill)
1275cc A-series High-performance Manual (Hammill)
Camshafts – How to Choose & Time Them For Maximum Power (Hammill)
Competition Car Datalogging Manual, The (Templeman)
Cylinder Heads, How to Build, Modify & Power Tune – Updated & Revised Edition (Burgess & Gollan)
Distributor-type Ignition Systems, How to Build & Power Tune – New 3rd Edition (Hammill)
Fast Road Car, How to Plan and Build – Revised & Updated Colour New Edition (Stapleton)
Ford SOHC 'Pinto' & Sierra Cosworth DOHC Engines, How to Power Tune – Updated & Enlarged Edition (Hammill)
Ford V8, How to Power Tune Small Block Engines (Hammill)
Harley-Davidson Evolution Engines, How to Build & Power Tune (Hammill)
Holley Carburetors, How to Build & Power Tune – Revised & Updated Edition (Hammill)
Honda Civic Type R High-Performance Manual, The (Cowland & Clifford)
Jaguar XK Engines, How to Power Tune – Revised & Updated Colour Edition (Hammill)
Land Rover Discovery, Defender & Range Rover – How to Modify Coil Sprung Models for High Performance & Off-Road Action (Hosier)
MG Midget & Austin-Healey Sprite, How to Power Tune – New 3rd Edition (Stapleton)
MGB 4-cylinder Engine, How to Power Tune (Burgess)
MGB V8 Power, How to Give Your – Third Colour Edition (Williams)
MGB, MGC & MGB V8, How to Improve – New 2nd Edition (Williams)
Mini Engines, How to Power Tune On a Small Budget – Colour Edition (Hammill)
Motorcycle-engined Racing Car, How to Build (Pashley)
Motorsport, Getting Started in (Collins)
Nissan GT-R High-performance Manual, The (Gorodji)
Nitrous Oxide High-performance Manual, The (Langfield)
Race & Trackday Driving Techniques (Hornsey)
Retro or classic car for high performance, How to modify your (Stapleton)
Rover V8 Engines, How to Power Tune (Hammill)
Secrets of Speed – Today's techniques for 4-stroke engine blueprinting & tuning (Swager)
Sportscar & Kitcar Suspension & Brakes, How to Build & Modify – Revised 3rd Edition (Hammill)
SU Carburettor High-performance Manual (Hammill)
Successful Low-Cost Rally Car, How to Build a (Young)
Suzuki 4x4, How to Modify For Serious Off-road Action (Richardson)
Tiger Avon Sportscar, How to Build Your Own – Updated & Revised 2nd Edition (Dudley)
TR2, 3 & TR4, How to Improve (Williams)
TR5, 250 & TR6, How to Improve (Williams)
TR7 & TR8, How to Improve (Williams)
V8 Engine, How to Build a Short Block For High Performance (Hammill)
Volkswagen Beetle Suspension, Brakes & Chassis, How to Modify For High Performance (Hale)
Volkswagen Bus Suspension, Brakes & Chassis for High Performance, How to Modify – Updated & Enlarged New Edition (Hale)
Weber DCOE, & Dellorto DHLA Carburetors, How to Build & Power Tune – 3rd Edition (Hammill)

RAC handbooks

Caring for your car – How to maintain & service your car (Fry)
Caring for your car's bodywork and interior (Sahota)
How your car works (Linde)

Those Were The Days ... Series

Alpine Trials & Rallies 1910-1973 (Pfundner)
Brighton National Speed Trials (Gardiner)
British Drag Racing – The early years (Pettitt)
Dune Buggy Phenomenon, The (Hale)
Dune Buggy Phenomenon Volume 2, The (Hale)
Endurance Racing at Silverstone in the 1970s & 1980s (Parker)
Hot Rod & Stock Car Racing in Britain in the 1980s (Neil)
Motor Racing at Brands Hatch in the Seventies (Parker)
Motor Racing at Brands Hatch in the Eighties (Parker)
Motor Racing at Crystal Palace (Collins)
Motor Racing at Goodwood in the Sixties (Gardiner)
Motor Racing at Nassau in the 1950s & 1960s (O'Neil)
Motor Racing at Oulton Park in the 1960s (McFadyen)
Motor Racing at Oulton Park in the 1970s (McFadyen)
Motor Racing at Thruxton in the 1970s (Grant-Braham)
Motor Racing at Thruxton in the 1980s (Grant-Braham)
Superprix – The Story of Birmingham Motor Race (Page & Collins)
Three Wheelers (Bobbitt)

Biographies

Amédée Gordini ... a true racing legend (Smith)
André Lefebvre, and the cars he created at Voisin and Citroën (Beck)
Cliff Allison, The Official Biography of – From the Fells to Ferrari\ (Gauld)
Edward Turner – The Man Behind the Motorcycles (Clew)
Jack Sears, The Official Biography of – Gentleman Jack (Gauld)
Jim Redman – 6 Times World Motorcycle Champion: The Autobiography (Redman)
John Chatham – 'Mr Big Healey' – The Official Biography (Burr)
The Lee Noble Story (Wilkins)
Pat Moss Carlsson Story, The – Harnessing Horsepower (Turner)
Tony Robinson – The biography of a race mechanic (Wagstaff)
Virgil Exner – Visioneer: The Official Biography of Virgil M Exner Designer Extraordinaire (Grist)

General

Alpine & Renault – The Development of the Revolutionary Turbo F1 Car 1968 to 1979 (Smith)
Alpine & Renault – The Sports Prototypes 1963 to 1969 (Smith)
Alpine & Renault – The Sports Prototypes 1973 to 1978 (Smith)
Autodrome (Collins & Ireland)
Autodrome 2 (Collins & Ireland)
Automotive A-Z, Lane's Dictionary of Automotive Terms (Lane)
Bluebird CN7 (Stevens)
British at Indianapolis, The (Wagstaff)
Cobra – The Real Thing! (Legate)
Cortina – Ford's Bestseller (Robson)
Daily Mirror 1970 World Cup Rally 40, The (Robson)
Drive on the Wild Side, A – 20 Extreme Driving Adventures From Around the World (Weaver)
Fast Ladies – Female Racing Drivers 1888 to 1970 (Bouzanquet)
Ford Cleveland 335-Series V8 engine 1970 to 1982 – The Essential Source Book (Hammill)
Ford GT – Then, and Now (Streather)
Ford GT40 (Legate)
Formula 5000 Motor Racing, Back then ... and back now (Lawson)
Forza Minardi! (Vigar)
GT – The World's Best GT Cars 1953-73 (Dawson)
Hillclimbing & Sprinting – The Essential Manual (Short & Wilkinson)
Intermeccanica – The Story of the Prancing Bull (McCredie & Reisner)
Kris Meeke – Intercontinental Rally Challenge Champion (McBride)
Lancia Delta HF Integrale (Blaettel & Wagner)
Le Mans Panoramic (Ireland)
Lola – The Illustrated History (1957-1977) (Starkey)
Lola – All the Sports Racing & Single-seater Racing Cars 1978-1997 (Starkey)
Lola T70 – The Racing History & Individual Chassis Record – 4th Edition (Starkey)
Lotus 49 (Oliver)
Mazda MX-5/Miata 1.6 Enthusiast's Workshop Manual (Grainger & Shoemark)
Mazda MX-5/Miata 1.8 Enthusiast's Workshop Manual (Grainger & Shoemark)
Mazda MX-5 Miata: The Book of the World's Favourite Sportscar (Long)
Mazda MX-5 Miata Roadster (Long)
Mini Minor to Asia Minor (West)
Motor Movies – The Posters! (Veysey)
Motor Racing – Reflections of a Lost Era (Carter)
Motor Racing – The Pursuit of Victory 1930-1962 (Carter)
Motor Racing – The Pursuit of Victory 1963-1972 (Wyatt/Sears)
Nissan 300ZX & 350Z – The Z-Car Story (Long)
Nissan GT-R Supercar: Born to race (Gorodji)
Rallye Sport Fords: The Inside Story (Moreton)
Roads with a View – England's greatest views and how to find them by road (Corfield)
Roads With a View – Wales' greatest views and how to find them by road (Corfield)
Supercar, How to Build your own (Thompson)
Toyota Celica & Supra, The Book of Toyota's Sports Coupés (Long)
Toyota MR2 Coupés & Spyders (Long)

From Veloce Publishing's new imprints:

BATTLE CRY!

Soviet General & field rank officer uniforms: 1955 to 1991 (Streather)
Red & Soviet military & paramilitary services: female uniforms 1941-1991 (Streather)

Hubble & Hattie

A comprehensive guide for the Trainee Dog Groomer (Gould & Ferguson)
A dog's dinner – Practical, healthy and nutritious recipes for REAL dog food (Paton-Ayre)
Animal Grief – How animals mourn for each other (Alderton)
Bramble: the dog who wanted to live forever (Heritage)
Cat Speak – recognising and understanding behaviour (Rauth-Widmann)
Clever Dog! – life lessons from the world's most successful animal (O'Meara)
Complete Dog Massage Manual, The – Gentle Dog Care (Robertson)
Dieting with my dog – one busy life, two full figures ... and unconditional love (Frezon)
Dinner with Rover – Delicious, nutritious meals for you and your dog to share (Paton-Ayre)
Dog Cookies (Schops)
Dog-friendly Gardening (Bush)
Dog Games – Stimulating play to entertain your dog and you (Blenski)
Dogs on wheels – Travelling with your canine companion (Mort)
Dog Relax – Relaxed dogs, relaxed owners (Pilguj)
Dog Speak – recognising and understanding behaviour (Blenski)
Emergency first aid for dogs – Home and away (Bucksch)
Exercising your puppy: a gentle & natural approach – Gentle Dog Care (Robertson)
Fun and games for cats! (Seidl)
Know Your Dog – The guide to a beautiful relationship (Birmelin)
Life skills for puppies – Laying the foundation for a loving, lasting relationship (Mills & Zulch)
Living with an Older Dog – Gentle Dog Care (Alderton & Hall)
Miaow! Cats really are nicer than people! (Moore)
My dog has arthritis ... but lives life to the full! (Carrick)
My dog has cruciate ligament injury – but lives life to the full! (Häusler)
My dog has hip dysplasia – but lives life to the full! (Häusler)
My dog is blind – but lives life to the full! (Horsky)
My dog is deaf – but lives life to the full! (Willms)
Partners (Walton)
Smellorama – nose games for dogs (Theby)
Swim to recovery: Canine hydrotherapy healing (Wong)
The truth about wolves and dogs – Dispelling the myths of dog training (Shelbourne)
Waggy Tails & Wheelchairs (Epp)
Walking the dog – motorway walks for drivers and dogs (Rees)
Walking the dog – French motorway walks for drivers and dogs (Rees)
Winston ... the dog who changed my life (Klute)
You and Your Border Terrier – The Essential Guide (Alderton)
You and Your Cockapoo – The Essential Guide (Alderton)

www.veloce.co.uk

First published in 2002, updated and revised edition in 2004 and January 2012 by Veloce Publishing Limited, Veloce House, Parkway Farm Business Park, Middle Farm Way, Poundbury, Dorchester, Dorset, DT1 3AR, England. Fax 01305 250479/e-mail info@veloce.co.uk/web www.veloce.co.uk or www.velocebooks.com.
ISBN: 978-1-845844-33-2 UPC: 6-36847-04433-6

Readers with ideas for automotive books, or books on other transport or related hobby subjects, are invited to write to the editorial director of Veloce Publishing at the above address. British Library Cataloguing in Publication Data – A catalogue record for this book is available from the British Library. Typesetting, design and page make-up all by Veloce Publishing Ltd on Apple Mac. Printed in India by Replika Press.

SpeedPro Series

How to build

TIGER AVON or GTA

SPORTS CARS FOR ROAD OR TRACK

UPDATED & REVISED NEW EDITION

VELOCE PUBLISHING
THE PUBLISHER OF FINE AUTOMOTIVE BOOKS

Build YOUR own dream sports car on a small budget! • Based mainly on Ford Sierra mechanical components • Choose your own engine, including Ford Pinto OHC & Zetec or other 4-cylinder engines • Includes chassis drawings • GRP manufacturing & fabrication • Car assembly • Now includes conversion of an existing Avon to a GTA

Contents

978-1-901295-26-9 978-1-903706-72-5 978-1-845843-15-1 978-1-845840-05-1 978-1-845840-06-8 978-1-845840-19-8

978-1-845840-21-1 978-1-845840-23-5 978-1-845840-45-7 978-1-845840-73-0 978-1-845841-23-2 978-1-845841-42-3

978-1-845841-62-1 978-1-845841-86-7 978-1-845841-87-4 978-1-845842-07-9 978-1-845842-08-6 978-1-845842-62-8

978-1-845842-66-6 978-1-845842-89-5 978-1-845842-97-0 978-1-845843-55-7 978-1-845844-14-1 978-1-845844-33-2

978-1-874105-70-1 978-1-903706-17-6 978-1-903706-59-6 978-1-903706-68-8 978-1-903706-70-1 978-1-903706-75-6

978-1-903706-76-3 978-1-903706-77-0 978-1-903706-78-7 978-1-903706-80-0 978-1-903706-94-7 978-1-903706-99-2

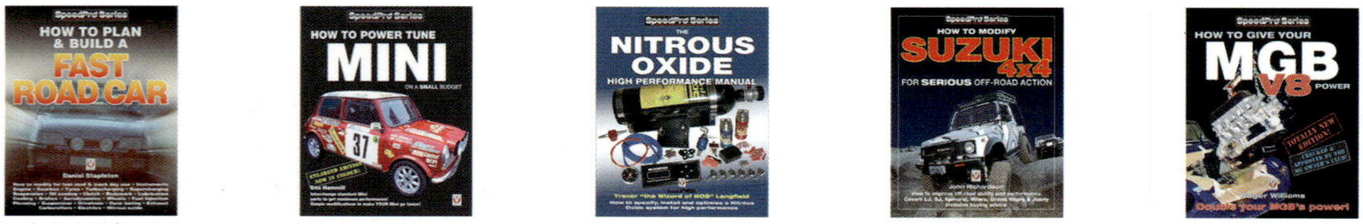

978-1-904788-78-2 978-1-904788-84-3 978-1-904788-89-8 978-1-904788-91-1 978-1-904788-93-5

'Teach them young!' Jim Dudley with grandson James.

car building, no matter whether the car is a Tiger Avon or not. There's even a chapter on mould making which means you can design and create your own unique bodywork, but still utilise the Tiger Avon chassis.

When you've completed your Tiger there's a thriving Tiger Club with various club meetings, track days and other events arranged throughout the year, Tiger even has its own UK race series with meetings throughout the season at most of the well known circuits, Within the club you'll meet new friends with like-minded enthusiasm for these sports cars.

THANKS

Over the years, I would hope that anyone who has visited Tiger Sportscars will have left with the impression of doing business with an enthusiastic and helpful family company.

Everybody at Tiger has an important part to play in the running of the business: Sue, my wife, puts up with me and helps out in general; Laura, my daughter, looks after parts and the Tiger Racing department; Paul, my son, manages workshop new builds and tuning; Gary manages the fabrication department; and Colin is technical and new builds.

My thanks must go to: Simon Ranson for much technical advice and technical drawings; Richard and Adam Wilkins and Giles Cooper for running the Tiger Owners' club and magazine; Giles Cooper also did the wiring drawings for the general manual, Tiger's manual and the Tiger Avon; last, but not least, Rod at Veloce Publishing.

Jim Dudley

Using this book & essential information

This book was been written with the help of Tiger sports car enthusiasts, some of whom have owned their cars for years. The book will give guidance and advice on all the various jobs you'll encounter during the build of your car.

When finished, if you're in the UK, the car will be required to pass the IVA (Individual Vehicle Approval) test and be issued with a certificate before you can register the car for road use through your local VRO (vehicle registration office); other countries may have equivalent schemes for self-built cars, so check with your local vehicle licensing authority.

The book includes information on donor vehicles, materials, skills, equipment, GRP (glass fibre reinforced plastic) mould making, body design, welding, general assembly, suspension settings and even racing your Tiger (should you so wish).

The car you build will be individual and it will be as good as you make it ... and you don't have to build it in the shortest possible time. Many of the Tigers I've seen have benefited from longer builds because their owners have taken more time to find the best solutions to the problems that inevitably occur during an individual build: in fact, I've seen some builders improve on the original Tiger specification! Realistically, as a minimum, it'll take something between 120-150 hours to build a Tiger Avon from a supplied chassis and bodykit. If you're building from scratch (including welding your own chassis and doing your own GRP work) then, of course, many more hours are going to be required.

Using the information in the GRP mould making chapter will allow you to design a completely different body shape from the standard Avon's, even something as different as the historic race car 'replicar' we produce (shown in some of the photos) which uses the same methods even though the body shape is much more complex.

USING THIS BOOK

Throughout this book the text assumes that you – or your contractor – will have workshop manuals (specific to the engine and other major donor components to be worked on) to follow for complete detail on dismantling, reassembly, adjustment procedure, clearances, torque figures, etc. This book's default for donor components is the standard manufacturer's specification so, if a procedure is not described, a measurement not given, a torque figure ignored, you can assume that the standard manufacturer's procedure or specification needs to be used for the relevant component. You can also phone Tiger's helpline if you need advice (see appendix).

You'll find it helpful to read the *whole* book *before* you start work or give instructions to your contractor.

This is because a modification or change in specification in one area will often cause the need for changes in other areas. Get the *whole* picture so that you can finalize specification and component requirements as far as is possible before any work begins.

References to the right-hand or left-hand side of the car are based on your perspective if you stand at the rear of the car and look forward.

ESSENTIAL INFORMATION

This book contains information on practical procedures; however, this information is intended only for those with the qualifications, experience, tools and facilities to carry out the work in safety and with appropriately high levels of skill. Whenever working on a car or component, remember that your personal safety must **ALWAYS** be your **FIRST** consideration. **The publisher, author, editors and retailer of this book cannot accept any responsibility for personal injury or mechanical damage which results from using this book, even if caused by errors or omissions in the information given. If this disclaimer is unacceptable to you, please return the pristine book to your retailer who will refund the purchase price.**

In the text of this book **'Warning!'** means that a procedure could cause personal injury and **'Caution!'** that there is danger of mechanical damage if appropriate care is not taken. However, be aware that we cannot possibly foresee every possibility of danger in every circumstance.

The importance of cleaning a component thoroughly before working on it cannot be overstressed. Always keep your working area and tools as clean as possible. Whatever specialist cleaning fluid or other chemicals you use, be sure to follow – completely – manufacturer's instructions and if you're using petrol (gasoline) or paraffin (kerosene) to clean parts, take every precaution necessary to protect your body and to avoid all risk of fire.

Important – All the technical drawings in this book are copyright and are intended to be used to produce a single Tiger Avon car. The drawings, photos and text are not to be photocopied, scanned or duplicated in any manner and are very strictly for private use. **Any use of information from this book for commercial purposes or unlicensed dissemination will lead to prosecution.**

Need Tiger's help?
E-mail – Jim@tigerracing.com

Safety, tools & FAQs

SAFETY

Warning! It is essential you read and understand this whole 'safety' section which contains important information regarding YOUR safety while you're working on your car. DO NOT regard this information as fully comprehensive because, as stated previously, we cannot foresee every threat to your safety so try to get into good habits with regard to working procedures and sensible precautions. For example, it's so easy to forget to wear goggles if you're sanding or grinding so perhaps, as a reminder, you can clip your goggles to the electric sander as you put your tools away?

Lifting

Never attempt to lift heavy components like engines and gearboxes, always use a engine hoist. Never lay under the car with the engine on the hoist.

Sanding

Always use a dust mask when sanding or working on your cars brake pads/shoes.

Body protection

Always wear goggles and protective gloves when sanding, grinding or hammering. Ditto, when there is a danger of chemical or battery acid splashes.

Before commencing work, remove finger rings, bracelets, loose clothing and tie back long hair. Shoes with toe protection are always a good idea.

If working with noisy devices, wear ear protection.

Proper body protection is absolutely vital when doing some jobs, such as goggles, gloves and ear protectors.

Clothing

Wear a good pair of fireproof overalls.

Fumes

Never run your engine in a confined space

When working with fuel (possibly draining petrol/gasoline) push the car into the open air to do the work and keep a fire extinguisher at hand.

Your car's battery gives off explosive hydrogen gas which is easily ignited, so be very careful when charging it.

Electrical

If your battery is short-circuited it can catch fire or explode!

Your car's ignition system can give you a very bad electrical shock.

Avoiding burns

Your car's exhaust system can get very hot and will take considerable time to cool!

If draining your radiator, let the engine cool first.

Ditto engine oil.

Battery acid will burn your skin, wash it off quickly with plenty of water if spilt.

Jacking

Never work on your car if it is supported by jacks. Make sure that adequately strong axle stands are supporting the chassis.

Here, the car is supported by a jack and an axle stand (jack stand). Never get under a car supported only by jacks.

Axle stands (jack stands). Make sure they have an appropriate weight capacity.

Children

Keep children away from your working area.

Sparks/flames

Remember when grinding, welding or testing ignition systems it's possible to ignite fuel or battery gases.

Always keep a suitable fire extinguisher near were you're working.

Paul working on a Tiger B6 fuel line: note the fire extinguisher nearby.

Electric tools

Do not use electric tools that have bad wiring. Do not use mains powered electric tools on wet components or when floors are wet.

Tools

Keep your tools in good condition, an ill-fitting screwdriver or spanner can slip ...

Time

Try to let someone know where you are and how long you're likely to be working on your car if you're working alone.

TOOLS

First of all, if you don't have all the tools mentioned here, especially the more unusual ones, you can hire what you need.

Most readers will have basic tools like a set of sockets and a set of spanners (these should be metric). If you're going to weld your own chassis a MIG welder is required. When installing the engine and gearbox an engine hoist will be required. A good vice is an essential tool.

If you don't have some of the tools listed and you want to keep costs down, try one or two local car boot fairs (flea markets) for secondhand tools: they can produce really good

One of the portable frames upon which chassis are built at Tiger. This simple device is easy to construct and makes life easier.

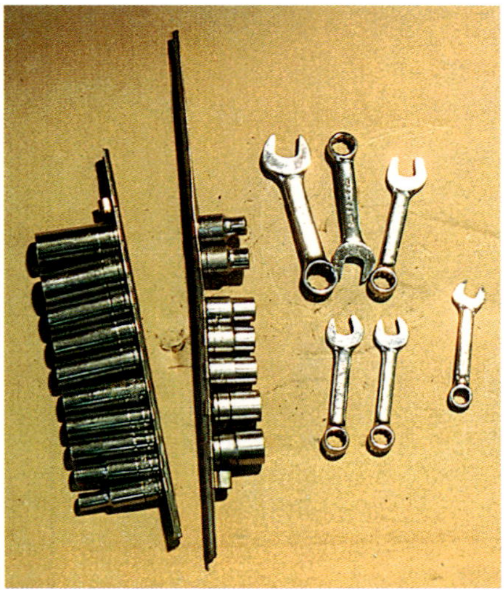

A selection of spanners (wrenches) and sockets.

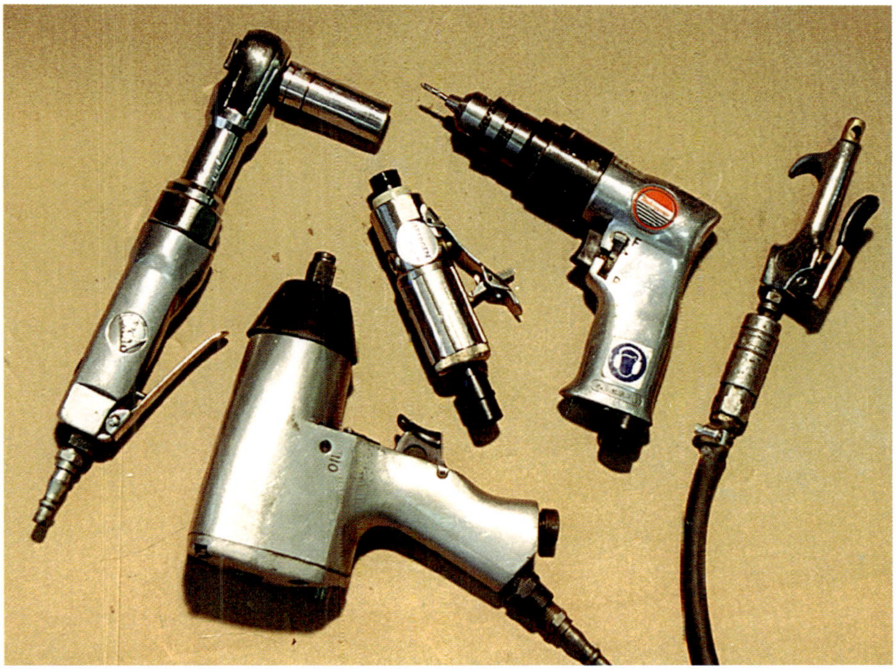

A selection of compressed air-powered tools.

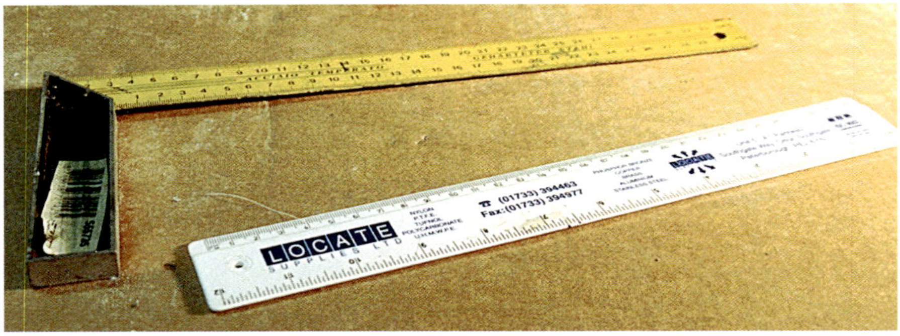

Set square and ruler.

Mole grips (vise grips).

Files and a wire brush.

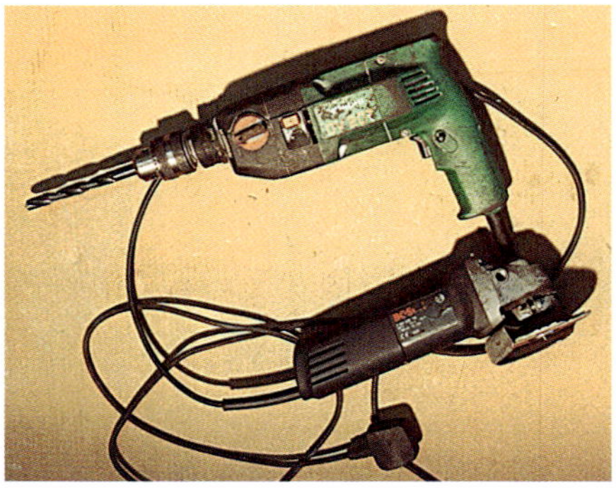

Electric drill and angle grinder.

Rubbing block for use with abrasive paper.

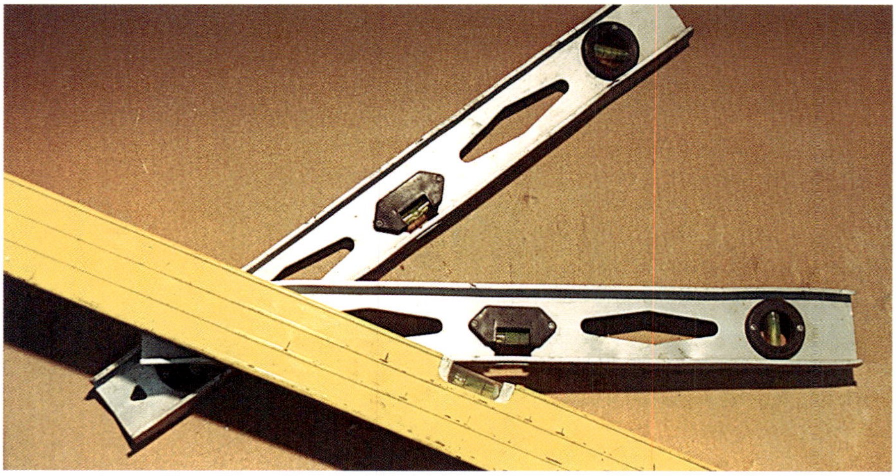

Spirit levels.

bargains. Another good source of new tools at reasonable prices are the trade stands at the various kit car and classic car shows throughout the year, these shows are also a good source of car parts for the self-builder.
Before you start your build, if you don't have a bench to work on, build one: you'll need it and, of course, the vice will fit on it!

At Tiger we use a rectangular frame to rest the chassis frame on as we start to build the car: we've put casters on each corner to make it easy to move the frame around.

Hand tools

The small hand tools most likely to be used over the build period are –

- Hacksaw
- Files
- Tin snips
- Pliers (regular type)
- Set square
- Tape measure
- Spirit levels (long and short)
- Marker pen
- Wire brush

Screwdriver set
Craft knife (Stanley-type)
Hammer

Hammer (soft-headed)
Mole grips (vise grips)
Clamps

Pop rivet (blind rivet) gun
Electric drill (mains electric)
Electric drill (portable rechargeable-type)
Drill bits
Small bench grinder (not essential)
Goggles
Gloves
Punch
Small angle grinder
Vice (vise)
Spanners (wrenches) and sockets

Tools for GRP work

Small containers (1 litre, or similar) for resin and gel coat
Selection of brushes
Selection or rollers
Stanley (craft) knife
Scissors
Marker pen
Plasticine
Rubbing block (for abrasive paper)

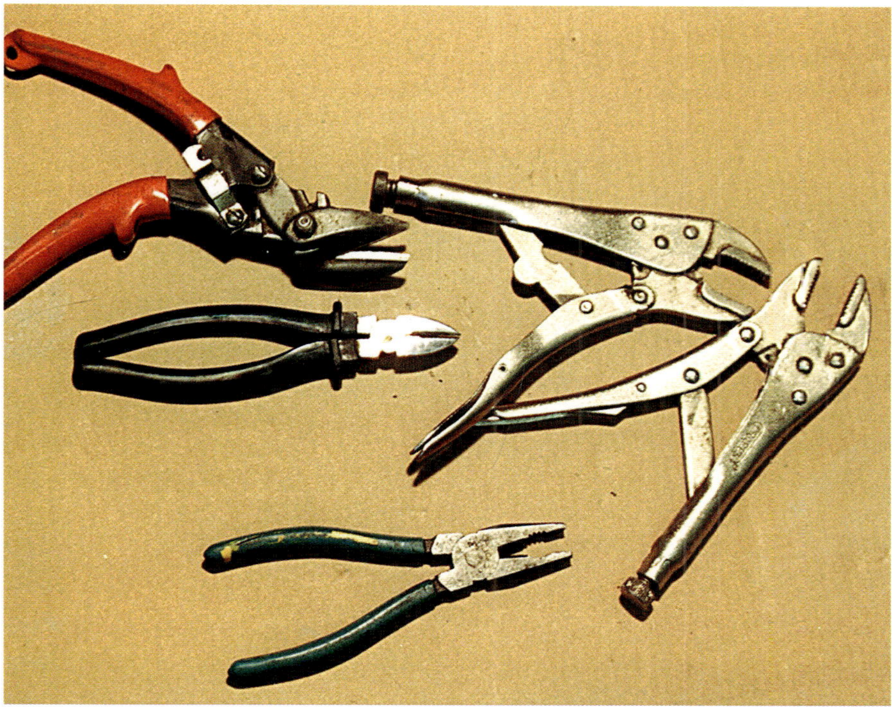

Pliers, wire cutter, sheet metal cutter and regular type Mole (vise) grips.

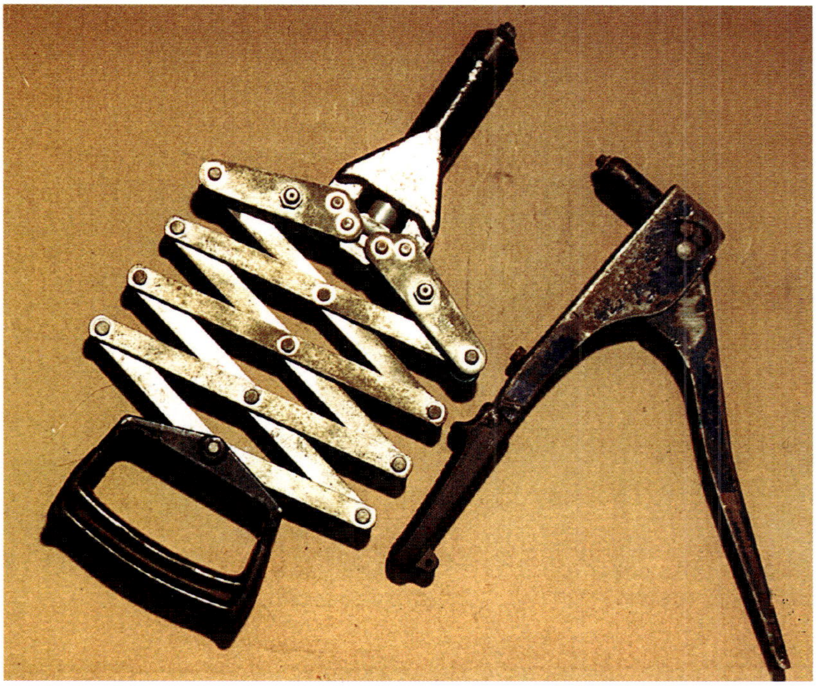

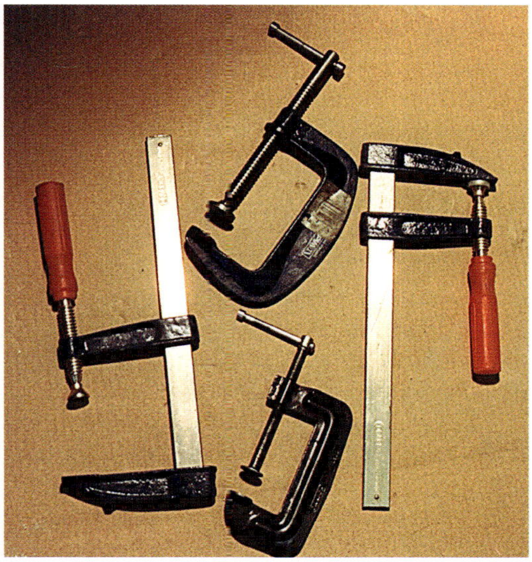

Various types of clamp.

Pop (blind) rivet guns.

FREQUENTLY ASKED QUESTIONS (FAQS)

Q: What engines can be fitted?
A: Most in-line four-cylinder engines can be fitted to the Tiger Avon, as can some V8 engines and 4-cylinder motorcycle units. The most commonly fitted engines now are Ford Zetec 16V, other taller engines may require a modification to the bonnet.

Q: Can engines from front-wheel drive cars be used?
A: Yes most Ford (Zetec) fwd (front-wheel drive) car engines will bolt onto a Ford Sierra (type 9) gearbox – some will need a new clutch, a new spigot bearing is pushed into the rear end of the crankshaft to support the gearbox input shaft in most cases. The Rover K-series can also be used in conjunction with the Sierra (Type 9) gearbox though a new convertor-type bellhousing will be required.

Q: Do the standard push-in rear driveshafts from the Sierra need to be modified in any way?
A: No.

Q: Does the standard Sierra propshaft need to be shortened?
A: Yes. **Warning!** it is essential to have this done by a professional engineer or purchase an Avon unit from Tiger. It's important that these propshafts are properly welded and balanced.

Q: Do I need to fit a catalytic converter in the exhaust system?
A: Not if the engine was manufactured in August 1995 or earlier (it's worth noting that the testing station will probably require proof of the manufacturing date of any engine). The August 1995 threshold applies to the UK; check with local vehicle testing authorities in other countries.

Q: If I use all new parts to build my car, will I receive a new (current) registration plate?
A: In the UK yes, but other countries may have different rules.

Q: Can I fit either type of front wings (fenders) to the Tiger Avon (long clam shell-type or cycle-type)?
A: Yes.

Q: Do I need a full windscreen (windshield) for the IVA test?
A: No, but *no* wipers/spindles/washers should be fitted. Again, this answer applies to the UK and other countries may have different rules.

Q: Can I paint the chassis or do I need to have it powder coated?
A: Yes, you can paint the chassis (with something like Smoothrite or Hammerite, or a tough paint suitable for chassis protection). Powder coating of the chassis and the suspension parts, like wishbones, also gives a durable finish.

Q: Can I use the wiring loom from the donor Ford Sierra?
A: Yes, but a new purpose made loom is recommended for much easier build (they're made to fit the much shorter car you're building and will make wiring much easier).

Q: Can I fit any brand/style of dashboard (fascia) instruments (dials)?
A: Usually you can, but the UK's IVA test limits the protrusion of instrument bezels and requires a minimum 2.5mm radius. So, when purchasing, order IVA compliant instruments, or plan how the instruments you want to use can be made compliant (bezels sunk in a thickly padded dashpanel surface or actually recessed into the dash, for instance).

Q: Do I need to fit a compensator valve in the rear brakes?
A: In most cases, yes. A good guide is if your donor car has it, fit it! The IVA requires approximately 25% of total braking effort to come from the rear brakes.

Q: Can I fit larger sidedraught (sidedraft) carburettors (ie: Weber/ Dellorto) to my pre-1995 engine?
A: Yes, but harmful exhaust emissions must remain within the statutory limit. This answer relates to the UK, other countries may have different requirements.

Q: Instead of buying a donor Ford Sierra, can I get all the donor car parts I need from Tiger Sportscars?
A: Yes, including rebuilt and tuned engines.

Need Tiger's help?
E-mail – Jim@tigerracing.com

Chapter 1
Component sources

Ford Sierra: the donor car for the Tiger Avon.

The Tiger Avon is designed to use donor parts sourced mainly from the Ford Sierra, a car built in huge numbers. However, you'll also need two front hubs and a steering rack from other Ford models and, maybe a windscreen wiper mechanism from a Mini (details of all major donor and aftermarket parts required will be found in this chapter).

Remember that, if necessary, all parts (including donor car parts) can be sourced directly from Tiger Sportscars.

SIERRA DONOR CAR PARTS

The specification of some Sierra components changed over time, the steering column varies in length, for example. However, allowance can be made for this difference when making the lower steering shaft (a new part needed to join the bottom of the Sierra column shaft to the steering rack).

Sierra wiper and indicator control stalk wiring connections vary, so make sure that when buying or stripping you

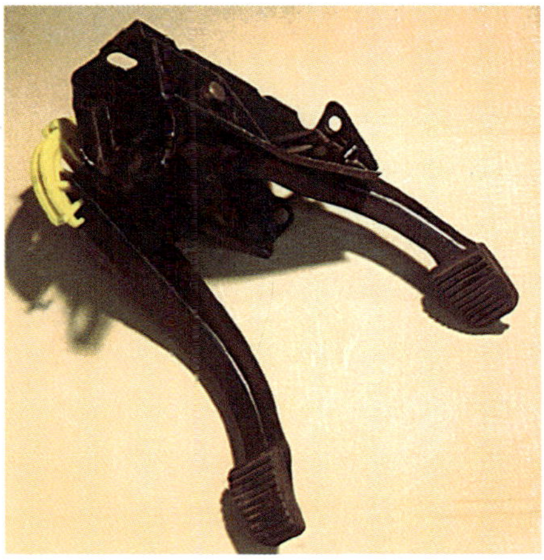

Sierra brake and clutch pedals can be used, usually with slight modification. These are in standard form.

Typical Ford Sierra steering column.

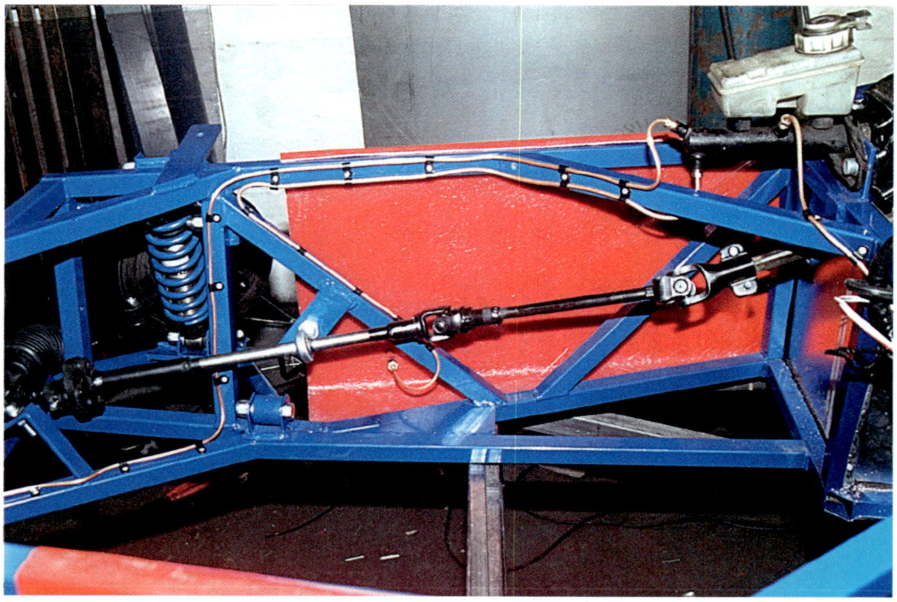

Modified (lengthened) Sierra steering shaft fitted to a Tiger chassis.

have the wiring plugs which push onto the stalks you intend to use.

Ford Sierra pedals can be used with slight modification, if floor-mounted pedals are your preference. A plate with a minimum thickness of 3.2mm (⅛in) must be bolted to the floor on which to mount the brackets that will pivot the floor pedals – you can find a picture in the chassis section on page 77.

Most donor cars will have covered many thousands of miles and, when it comes to reconditioning, most builders tend to think of the engine first. In fact, it's much better to make the brakes the first priority on your list of items to be bought new or reconditioned. Usually, if it's been decided that they're OK, the donor car gearbox and rear axle/differential unit components can simply be cleaned with a wire brush and, where appropriate, painted with special paints that can be applied direct to metal to give tough hammered, smooth and satin finishes. However, for a professional finish, sand blasting before painting (even better, powder coating), is best. At this stage, even if the oil seals on the gearbox look dry, change them anyway!

Checking donor car components

The best way of assessing the condition of the required components of the donor car is to drive the car before you buy it.

Engine & clutch

If it's not possible to drive the car you may still be able to start the engine. If so, when it's at normal running temperature look for oil smoke from the exhaust when the engine's revved. Check for valve guide wear by turning off the warm engine, restarting it after five minutes and immediately looking for blue smoke from the exhaust. Check oil pressure at the gauge if possible; if not, at least check that the oil pressure warning light is working OK and extinguishes as soon as the engine is running. Rev the engine and listen for rattles; try the clutch operation and note that, in general, a clutch that doesn't engage until the clutch pedal is close to the top of its travel is usually severely worn.

If you want to power tune a Sierra engine, you'll find excellent advice in another *SpeedPro* book – *How To Power Tune Ford SOHC 'Pinto' and Sierra Cosworth DOHC Engines*.

This Tiger B6 chassis has been powder coated for durable protection.

Wheels & tyres

Sierra wheels and tyres (tires) can be used if you're on a tight budget, though, of course, you can use new or secondhand alloy wheels and new tyres if you prefer. **Warning!** Used wheels and tyres must be in excellent condition. The Avon is designed for standard Ford Sierra offset wheels.

If you're going to use the donor car wheels, check that they're not buckled by spinning them and then holding a screwdriver blade as close to the exposed spinning rim edge as possible: if the rim doesn't stay a constant distance from the screwdriver, the wheel is buckled. Also check for kerbing damage, obvious cracks, and enlargement of the wheel nut holes caused by loose wheel nuts. Reject any wheel that seems less than perfect. Generally, secondhand tyres are not worthwhile unless they're relatively new (not age hardened), with no obvious damage and with plenty of evenly dispersed tread: as a precaution have them checked by one of those tyre and exhaust companies you find in every town.

Brakes

It's almost certain that you'll need to change the brake discs/drums and pads/shoes (new components are highly recommended). Also check the condition of the wheel cylinders/callipers for leaks. Note that some Sierras have rear wheel disc brakes which you may prefer, but you may need to modify the hub or bearing holder to fit these. **Warning!** Bear in mind that the car you're building will accelerate much quicker than the original Sierra (because it's lighter), so you need to be able to have absolute confidence in the brakes.

The handbrake lever is taken from the Sierra, or a 'trigger'-type could be used.

Rear axle components

The donor car's rear axle crownwheel & pinion/differential unit is unlikely to have any faults (in fact, the whole Sierra drivetrain is fairly reliable). To check the 'diff' unit, with the help of a assistant turn both the driveshafts in a forward direction simultaneously and check for smooth rotation; also make sure there is no sign of oil leakage past the three 'diff' unit (propshaft and driveshaft flanges) oil seals, and also the condition of the driveshaft gaiters. Again, it's worth changing these seals even if they look dry.

Some Sierra CV (constant velocity) joints have an outer diameter of 72mm, while others have an outside diameter of 73mm. The smaller type is better for the Tiger Avon, and will fit the upright (hub carrier) described in the book. However, the larger type can be accommodated by using an appropriately sized piece of tubing in the construction of the upright.

Steering column

On the steering column you'll need to check that the bush at the lower end is in good condition, and also the operation of the steering lock.

Ignition system

The ignition system from the Sierra engine can be used, though there are companies producing high-performance distributors better suited to aftermarket high-performance camshafts these days. Another book in the *SpeedPro* series – *How to Build & Power Tune Distributor-type Ignition Systems* – will tell you how to optimise ignition system performance and even how to modify standard distributors.

Wiring loom

The wiring loom from your donor Sierra can be used, but a bespoke loom for the Tiger Avon is strongly recommended as it's a better and much easier solution to wiring the new car you're building. There are

Ford Sierra rear axles including suspension arms, differential, driveshafts, rear hubs and rear brakes.

various companies producing looms for clubman-type cars at reasonable prices. You'll find wiring diagrams for the Avon elsewhere in this book. Note that the Avon uses a rocker switch fitted in the dash (fascia) rather than the standard Sierra side/headlamp stalk type switch which is cut off during the build.

NON-SIERRA PARTS

Read the chapter on Individual Vehicle Approval (IVA) before you start purchasing parts for your car and, if possible, purchase the IVA manual.

There are going to be a number of parts that you will not be able to take from the donor car: for instance, the donor Sierra will not have the preferred round instrument dials. When it comes to dashboard instruments and switches, remember that, in the UK, there are IVA requirements regarding how far both are allowed to protrude from the dash surface. If you're using gauges that are not IVA compliant, pad the dash more and/or inset dials and switches appropriately.

Alternative engine choices

Probably the best engine choice for the future is the Ford Zetec 16v unit (as fitted to the Ford Mondeo or Escort) which will also bolt onto the Sierra's 'Type 9' gearbox.

Another option is the Ford CVH engine (which will also bolt onto a Type 9 box) as fitted to the Ford Escort Mk3.

When adapting either of these two front-wheel drive engines to the Sierra gearbox, the clutch may need to be changed (usually only the centre plate) and you'll need to install a spigot bearing in the rear end of the crankshaft. The latter is an easy job that is done by gently tapping the new Sierra (manual gearbox) spigot bearing

Typical bag-type washer bottle installation above the pedal area.

into the end of the crankshaft using a socket of the same diameter as the bearing.

The older Ford crossflow 'Kent' engine will bolt straight onto the Ford Type 9 box from the Sierra, but these power units are getting harder to find as the years go by.

You can also use Rover K-series engines and various V8 engines, though you'll need a special bellhousing to mate these with the Ford Type 9 gearbox and, possibly, gearbox 1st motion shaft mods too.

If a V8 engine is your choice, allowances will have to be made in the tunnel chassis tubes during your build (if building your own chassis), or when ordering from Tiger.

Suitable motorcycle engines can be used to power the Tiger Avon and you'll find a chapter dedicated to this subject elsewhere in this book.

Rectangular-shaped aftermarket-type rear lights are easy to obtain.

Right-side indicator light on a clamshell-type wing (fender).

Suspension bushes

You'll need new aftermarket bushes (steel sleeve with rubber insert type), for your car's suspension (road use) or, for racing, you can use the nylon type.

It's worth remembering, though, that some race series will not let you use rose joints on suspension.

Windscreen wipers & washers

If you're using a full windscreen (windshield), you'll need a wiper motor and the two wiper wheelboxes (the parts that the wiper arms push onto), all of which can be sourced from a Mini.

You'll need a washer bottle or an aftermarket bag, but check the IVA regulations regarding the minimum amount of fluid required.

Lights

The headlight shells are usually of the chrome bowl type fitted with Mini-type sealed beam light units, though halogen bulbs can also be used.

You'll need aftermarket rear lamps and these can be of the round or rectangular type found quite cheaply at most motor factors and at automotive shows.

As well as headlights and rear lights (including brake lights), you'll need side indicators, rear foglamp, reversing lamp, front indicators, rear indicators and a rear number plate (licence plate) light.

Suspension units

Use aftermarket combined (coaxial) coil spring/telescopic shock absorber units with built-in adjustment for

You may need to mount the indicators on stalks to pass the UK's IVA test or similar legislation in other countries.

damping resistance and spring seat height.

Front suspension units: open length 298mm (11.75in), compressed length 260mm (10.25in). Note: if measured without a rubber bump stop, compressed length would be 235mm (9.25in). All measurements taken centre-to-centre of the mounting bush eyes. For spring data see appendices.

Rear suspension units: open length 349mm (13.75in), compressed length 285mm (11.25in). Note: if measured without a rubber bump stop, compressed length would be 260mm (10.25in). All measurements taken centre-to-centre of the mounting bush eyes. For spring data see appendices.

Telescopic suspension unit with adjustable damping (resistance) and a spring platform adjustable for height.

Steering rack

The steering rack is from a Ford Escort Mk2 and will need modification that extends the trackrod end from Escort to Cortina Mk 4/5 length. Alternatively, purpose-built new racks are available from Tiger. Quick racks are now becoming very popular, as more drivers are taking their cars on track days. These are usually around 2.5 turns lock-to-lock.

Trackrod ends and wishbone ball joints

The trackrod ends are Ford Escort Mk2 type, the top wishbone ball joint from the Ford Transit, while the lower wishbone ball joint is from the Fiat 124.

A standard Tiger radiator with electric fan (here fitted to a Tiger R6).

Radiator & electric fan

A new bespoke radiator will be needed and it will require an electric fan. You can find suitable electric fans fitted to the radiators of small hatchbacks.

All Tiger systems have the radiator thermo switch fitted on the top of the radiator.

Front suspension uprights/hubs

The front upright/stub axle/hub/brake disc assemblies are sourced from the Ford Cortina Mk4 & Mk5. New aftermarket units are also available.

Battery

A Sierra-type battery (45amp hour) is fine for the Avon, although, if a Zetec engine is being used, 55 amps is recommended.

Cortina upright complete with hub and brake disc fitted to a Tiger Avon.

Top: Cortina upright and hub with brake calliper removed.
Above: Cortina cast brake calliper – alloy aftermarket brake callipers are now being used in place of the older cast type.

If fitting alloy wheels, check that the wheel studs on your donor vehicle are long enough, and replace with longer studs as required.

Need Tiger's help?
E-mail – Jim@tigerracing.com

Chapter 2
Raw materials

If you're going to construct your own chassis, suspension wishbones and bodywork you'll need the raw materials detailed in the following lists. Of course, you can also obtain these items in kit or finished form direct from Tiger Sportscars.

CHASSIS

If building your own chassis, you'll need:
(Note that tubing should be ERW (Electric Resistance Welded) type).
1in (25.4mm) outside dimension square mild steel tube: 16swg thickness
0.75in (19mm) outside dimension square mild steel tube: 16swg thickness
1in (25.4mm) outside dimension square mild steel tube: 12swg thickness
1.5in x 0.75in (38.1 x 19mm) outside dimension steel tube: 16swg thickness
0.75in (19mm) outside diameter square mild steel tube: wall thickness 3.5mm
1.25in (32mm) outside diameter round mild steel tube: wall thickness 3.5mm

Pre-cut lengths of steel tubing at Tiger's workshop ready to be used for chassis construction.

⅛in (3.2mm) mild steel plate
40mm x 5mm mild steel plate
25mm x 5mm mild steel plate
40mm x 8mm mild steel plate

SUSPENSION

If building your own wishbones, you'll need:
1inch (25.4mm) outside diameter round mild steel tube: wall thickness 12swg (for all wishbones)
35mm outside diameter round tube: wall thickness 4mm (for bushes)
40mm x 5mm mild steel plate
40mm x 8mm mild steel plate
⅛in (3.2mm) mild steel plate

PANELS TO SEAL OFF COCKPIT FROM CHASSIS

Aluminium sheet 18-20swg thickness

GRP BODY

If you want to make your own body you'll need:
Resin (general purpose)
Glass fibre (450 grams per metre)
Catalysts (hardener)
Gel coat
Plastic release agent (general purpose)

Aluminium sheeting of various thicknesses in the Tiger workshops.

Mould release wax
Mutton cloth
Plasticine
Aluminium strips
Tank (Duck or Duct) tape
Masking tape
Cellulose thinners

PAINTWORK & GENERAL FINISHING

Wet & dry paper (180, 240, 400, 600 & 1000 grade)
Production paper (40-80 grade)
Primer
Top coat (either two pack or cellulose)
Stopper paste
Body filler
Cellulose thinners
Rubbing compound (fine)
Mutton cloth

MOULD MAKING

When you start drawing your body design ideas you'll find that you'll need to look at the various shapes required and how you can construct a mould to achieve a particular shape. You can even use an appropriately shaped object as a 'plug' to make a GRP female mould from. For example, if you wanted a curved section as part of a particular shape, you could look at the U-shape of plastic rainwater guttering to be incorporated into the mould you're building. Do you get the idea?

There are so many different types of materials that can be used depending on what shapes you want to create. The following are just a few we've used over the years at Tiger Sportscars -

Wood in rectangular and square section
Wood in round section (*eg*: broom stick or dowel)
Car rubber heater hose
Plywood (flat)
Aluminium sheet (20swg and 16swg)
GRP wing from an old trailer (modified)
Polystyrene foam
Wood veneer
Flat plastic strip
Flat glass
Round plastic pipe (small and large)
Vinyl material (stuck to mould for material look in interior)

Stopper paste.

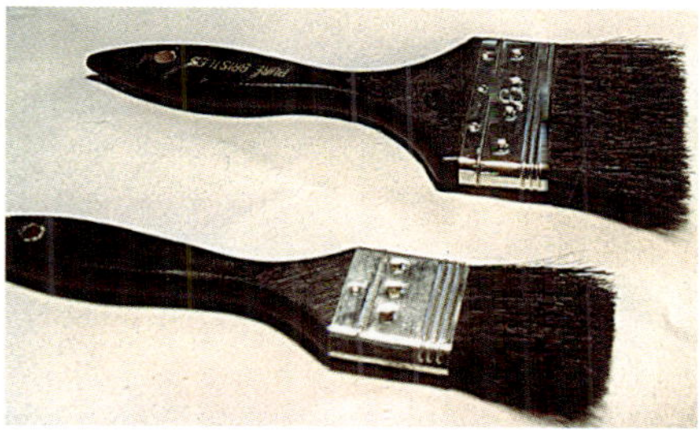

Pure bristle paint brushes.

Paint spray guns. The smaller one is used for primer, the larger one for finish coats.

Body filler with hardener packs.

Mould (mold) release wax.

Duck (duct) and masking tape.

Perspex
Various rear spoilers from production cars (use only certain parts of the shape)
Glasses (drinking) for rear lamp shapes in your mould
Plaster
Clay
Bodyfiller
Flat GRP sections
Cardboard (shape, then cover in bodyfiller)

Chapter 3
GRP bodywork

INTRODUCTION TO GRP

GRP (glassfibre reinforced polyester or plastic), often called 'fibreglass' or just 'glass,' is used in many industries. GRP is ideal for low volume production runs and one-off shapes, so most medium to small car companies use this material extensively.

To cure the resin an amount of catalyst (hardening agent) in correct proportion to the amount of resin is mixed into it. The mix cures better with the application of a small amount of heat, so most laminating is carried out in workshops with temperatures of around 60-65 degrees.

A gel coat, which can be coloured or clear, is applied to the mould after the release agents. Next, the glass mat is laid onto the gel coat and then the resin is brushed onto the glass and rolled out with a 'paddle' roller: the rolling procedure is intended to remove all trapped air.

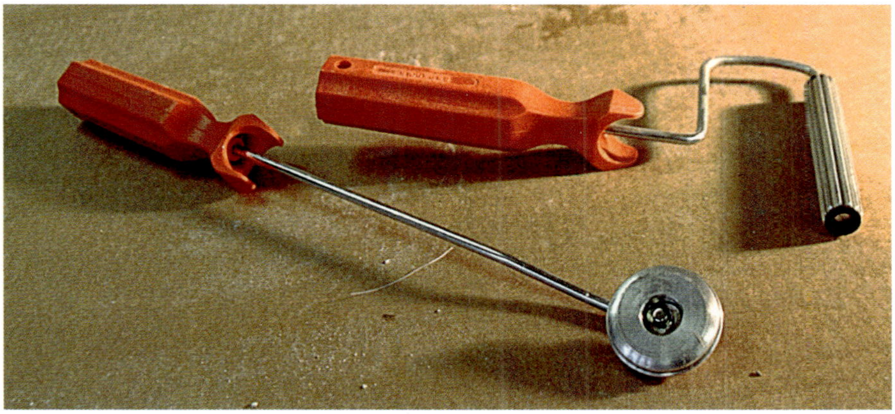

Paddle rollers.

DESIGNING STRONG GRP STRUCTURES

GRP is very strong, especially when made into three-dimensional shapes, such as box sections – these structures can then be fixed to other structures to give even greater strength. For example, the Lotus Elan used a steel backbone chassis with a GRP body bolted to it at various points. You can also fix a GRP box section behind a flat, or relatively flat, GRP section and laminate the two together to produce much more strength. This technique is often used on sill (rocker) panels on GRP bodywork.

Essentially, GRP gives the designer a freedom that is very difficult to achieve with other materials, such as aluminium or steel.

The Tiger 250 model mould with various bolted flanges that allow it to be split.

USEFUL TIPS FOR DESIGNING & MAKING GRP PANELS

- Always roll out the resin soaked glassfibre with a purpose made roller. **Caution! Do not** be tempted to try and do the job with a brush.
- **Caution!** Always mix in the **correct percentage** of catalyst, as stated by the manufacturer.
- When designing your shapes try to retain a radius on most edges of 5mm (0.20in) minimum. If applicable, also check radii required for IVA.
- Look carefully at your design and realise that shapes which have areas wider than the opening in the mould through which they will be withdrawn will mean that the mould must be splittable (ie: mould parts bolted together).
- One-piece moulds must have a minimum of 3 degrees of taper so that the mould exit is always larger than any part of the interior (otherwise you will not be able to extract the moulded item).
- Generally, the thickness of the gel coat lay up should be around 2mm (0.08) – two coats should be applied using a brush, and apply an extra coat over the joint in split moulds. Older moulds may need slightly thicker gel coats if they have worn over the years and have one or two surface defects (which will result in marks in the finished product). However, a thicker gel can be flatted and polished to remove such flaws without breaking through to the fibreglass beneath. Of course, there's really no substitute for a good mould with no imperfections.
- Aim for a finished lay-up with glass of around 4-5mm thick (including gel coat) when cured. This thickness usually comprises two layers of fibreglass matting, but actually depends on the thickness of glass being used. **Caution!** If you're going to use three sheets of matting, watch out for overheating (leave to cool slightly between layers). Thicker lay-ups will be heavier.
- When mixing the gel or resin the quantity of catalyst to be added is usually between 3 and 6 per cent. It is **essential** that you follow the manufacturer's instructions regarding the amount of catalyst to be used. However, don't forget that heat will set the mix quicker so, if your workshop is hot, it's more than likely that the catalyst quantity can be towards the minimum recommended amount.

Catalyst or 'hardener' causes liquid resin to harden.

For new moulds it's also a good precaution to apply PVA (Polyvinyl Alcohol) release agent.

After a small gap is opened with a soft wooden wedge, warm soapy water can be poured between mould and panel to aid release.

BRUSHES & ROLLERS

You'll need a small selection of brushes (25, 50 & 75mm/1, 2 & 3in) and rollers (25, 50 & 100mm/1, 2 & 4in), pots, thinners or acetone, and a good system of keeping your brushes clean and usable. One way of keeping brushes in good condition is to obtain 3 pots and fill each with thinners or acetone. The first pot is for the contaminated brush to be initially cleaned, then clean it again in the second pot. Finally, leave the brush suspended in the third pot so that the bristles are immersed. After a time the first pot will be badly contaminated so dispose of it and move the second pot to first, the third pot now becomes the second and a new third pot is filled with clean thinners/acetone. You can use exactly the same method to keep rollers in good condition.

RELEASE AGENTS

Before making any parts in a mould a release agent of some kind will need to be applied to the mould: generally the release agent is in the form of a mould release wax. This wax is applied 4 or 5 times to new moulds and moulds which have not been used for a while. When applying the wax **always** allow to dry before polishing with a good quality mutton cloth and, if possible, leave the last coat of wax to dry overnight before polishing.

For new moulds it's also a good precaution (at least for the first pull out) to apply PVA (Polyvinyl Alcohol) release agent after the 5 waxes. Use a small sponge to apply the PVA.

If on the first pull the GRP panel that you have just laid up inside the mould is difficult to remove, small wooden wedges can be driven gently between the mould and GRP panel. Warm soapy water can also be tipped between mould and panel to free the panel. Gently tapping with a rubber hammer can also assist the first pull from a new mould. **Caution!** Do not use excessive force to free a panel from the mould or you may damage the panel's gel coat.

Generally, once there has been one 'pull' from a new mould it can be cleaned and rewaxed and will be OK for all future pulls as long as it is waxed from time to time.

The term 'green GRP' refers to GRP that has not yet cured properly: in fact, complete curing can take days even though the new part looks hard and perfectly formed much sooner than this. If the new GRP panel has been taken from the mould too early it's probably still 'green' and this means that it can change shape – even distort badly – as it continues to cure in an unsupported state. **Caution!** Leave your new GRP panels in the mould for as long as you can, but at least a minimum of two days to cure.

Split moulds can sometimes allow the gel coat to seep into their joints, a

'Chopped strand' glassfibre, useful for tight corners.

layer of Plasticine (squashed between the joint or smoothed into it) will help to give a better 'flash line' (ridge on the finished panel). Small flash lines on the finished panel can be sanded and polished out.

Damaged edges on split moulds, or on the radiused edges of one-piece moulds, can be temporarily repaired using Plasticine. However, for a better and much more permanent repair drill the damaged area to a depth of approximately halfway into the thickness of the mould, mix a small amount of gel and apply to the hole leaving the new gel repair with a slightly raised surface. Leave for 24 hours then gently sand the repair surface using progressively finer abrasive papers from 240 grit 'wet and dry' to 800 grit. Use soap and water to lubricate the abrasive paper. The gel can now be polished first with a paint cutting compound then a mild car paintwork surface reviver. Finally, wax the repair five times.

For tricky moulds that have small radii around their edges, or tight corners which are difficult to get into with the roller, try using 'chopped strands': these are glassfibre strands (usually 10mm-15mm long) which can be mixed into a small pot of resin and applied into tight corners/radii. Sheet glassfibre can then be rolled over or into the strands. To strengthen a large area, like the underside of a bonnet (hood), lay a 'core mat' into the second layer: this material will give strength and lightness.

For best results when laying down and rolling your glassfibre matting, always try to roll it out in the mould as close to horizontal as possible. This is because, if you lay and roll out the glassfibre matting in a vertical or semi vertical position, resin will tend to run downward and puddle in the bottom of the mould which can leave air in the lay-up with the puddles getting too warm and curing too quickly. To allow the matting to be laid out as close to horizontal as possible, it's best to build 'rotatability' into your mould design which can easily be done when making it by incorporating flats or legs to allow it to be turned and to be stable in several orientations.

If you're designing or making a GRP section or panel that is to be bolted to a steel chassis you can bond a steel reinforcement plate (to be drilled) or purpose made bobbins (with either bolt holes or threaded studs) into the GRP when laying your glassfibre matting into the mould.

Make paper patterns for the glass matting shapes needed before you start rolling out: this will help you get matting of a more consistent thickness by avoiding unnecessary overlaps.

SAFETY

Warning! When working with GRP **always** wear eye protection, and when sanding **always** wear a dust mask. **Warning!** When mixing the resin and laying up the glassfibre make sure the room or workshop is very well ventilated.

Most resins have a certain amount of accelerator already mixed into them when purchased so that as soon as you add the catalyst the curing begins. Additional accelerator can be added but, in general, is not needed (follow the manufacturer's instructions on this subject). **Warning!** Never mix accelerator with the catalyst as the mix can be explosive and can result in fire.

MAKING A MOULD FROM A PLUG

When working on complex shapes and curves the mould will usually need to be split in one or more places. This

Mould (mold) release wax and mutton cloth.

will definitely be the case if any part of the moulded shape is wider than the opening in the mould through which the finished cured panel will have to be pulled out. To produce a good mould from a plug (a shape to be replicated) the plug needs to have a good surface which must be highly polished and, in most cases, mould release wax applied, dried and polished through 5 applications.

If you're creating a mould which requires a splitting flange because of its shape, the flange is best put on at the stage when the plug has otherwise just been finished and is in polished condition

Decide where you're going to put the flange and what material you're going to use to make the upstand that will create the flange. A typical way of making the flange former is to use a piece of wood shaped to match the contours of the plug and which will usually be held in place by a series of screws (and possibly small angle brackets). The problem with this system is that after you lay-up the mould with its GRP flange in the first part of the plug, let it cure and remove the wooden flange former, there are holes left in the plug from the screws! You'll now have to repair the screw holes before laying up the second part of the moulded panel ...

Another method for making flanges is to use 20swg aluminium sheet. First make a cardboard template to establish the exact shape required, then transfer the shape of the template to the alloy. Next hold the shaped aluminium sheet in place (at a 90 degree angle to the plug) and tank/duct tape its underside to the plug (the taped side will not be used in the first lay-up). Now seal the joint between the alloy flange former and the plug with Plasticine and smooth it off using a plastic spreader (from your body filler).

Apply, dry and polish 5 coats of mould wax. Apply a coat of PVA release agent and let it dry (Drawing 3.1, stage 1).

The gel coat can now be applied (Drawing 3.1, stage 2) and when it's dried to a tacky finish you can lay up the first layer of GRP matting.

Let the first layer of GRP dry (leaving it for two hours at least) then lay up more layers (Drawing 3.1, stage 3), but allowing the mould to cool between each coat. Usually 4 or 5 layers of matting will be fine for a mould with one or two more applied at the flanges.

Once you've finished the first side of the mould and it has cured, the alloy flange former and tape can be removed (Drawing 3.1, stage 4).

You may need to clean up the plug surface where the tape that secured the

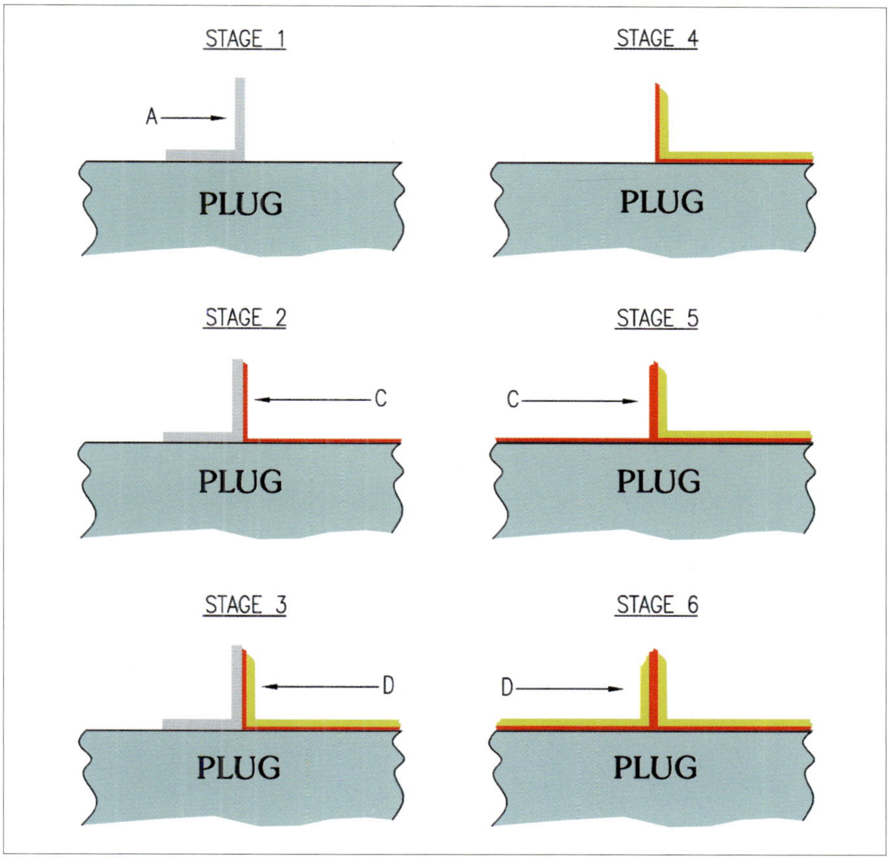

Drg 3.1 – How to form flanges in six stages. Stage 1: A = Flange (in alloy or other material). Stage 2: C = Gel coat. Stage 3: D = GRP lay-up. Stage 4: Non-GRP flange (A) removed. Stage 5: C = Gel coat applied to GRP flange and plug. Stage 6: D = GRP lay-up over second part of plug and GRP flange.

flange was and this can be done with thinners – be careful not to damage the finish when cleaning. Apply release wax to the second part of the plug, including the new GRP flange and polish off in the normal way. Apply PVA release to the new GRP flange.

Apply gel coat to the second part of the plug including the flange (Drawing 3.1, stage 5) followed by GRP matting (Drawing 3.1, stage 6). In fact, the procedure for making the second half of the mould is the same as for the first part.

When a split mould is parted after moulding a panel, wash it with warm soapy water to remove the PVA coating.

If you find that there are some marks left by the use of the PVA these can be flatted and polished using 400 grade followed by 1000 grade wet and dry abrasive paper, polishing with paint cutting compound, polishing further with a mild paintwork restorer like T-Cut and then finishing with 5 applications of mould release wax. For the first subsequent panel moulding also add a coat of PVA just to be safe. After the first panel you should just be able to gel and lay up for a further 5 'pulls' before having to repeat the clean up procedure.

The accompanying photographs show the full sequence of making/preparing plugs, making moulds and then moulding finished panels. The pictures, which illustrate general principles, relate to the English Racing Automobiles racing single seater, the Tiger Storm and Tiger Avon.

Tom cutting out the shaped plywood armatures for front and rear of tub (ERA).

Paul fixing wooden strips to the shaped plywood armatures (English Racing Automobiles single-seater).

Above & right: Glue being applied to the body formers to hold the thin sheets of wood veneer which are also stapled.

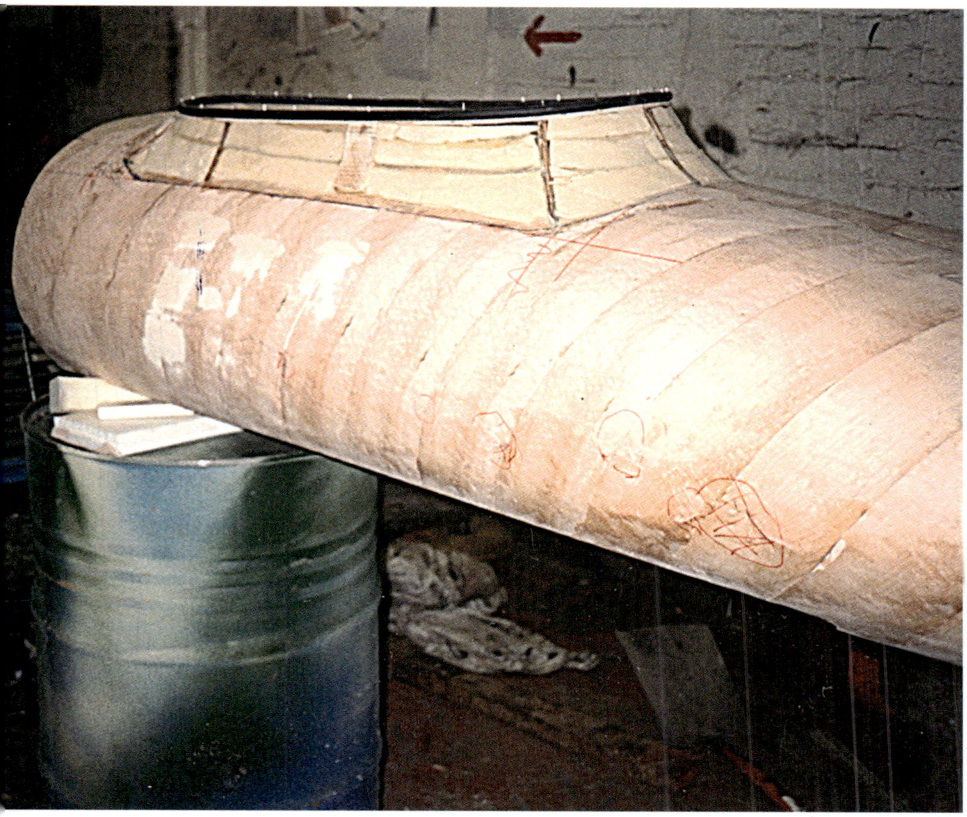

Above, left & next page, top: The finished shape.

Another example of making a plug (rear of the Tiger Storm) ...

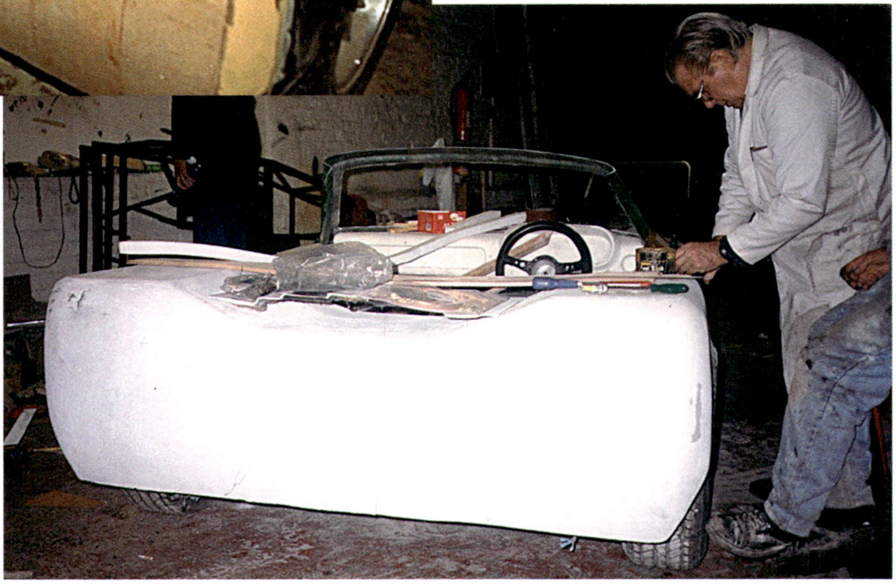

... fine-tuning the shape and surface finish of the plug ...

... the moulded body itself.

Building a plug for the front bodywork of the Tiger Storm, and the ...

... finished product.

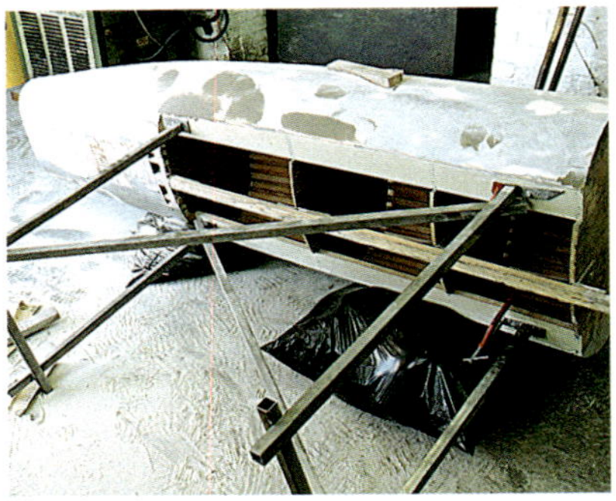

It's now time to make a stand for the racing single-seater's plug which will make further work much easier.

Apply a layer of body filler.

For the first rough smoothing of the filler a heavy-duty sander can be used, but make sure you follow the safety rules.

Time for the harder work: rubbing down by hand (the only way to get a really good finish). Use production paper, working down through progressively finer grades before the primer is applied.

A guide coat of paint spray will show up the low spots as you rub down.

Once the shape and surface are OK, apply a heavy coat of primer ...

... use stopper filler to fill any remaining low spots.

After spraying with top coat, 'flat' (smooth) the surface with wet & dry paper (nothing coarser than 600 grit), using soap and water to lubricate the paper.

The nose of the racer being wet flatted.

To get the plug surface really smooth use paint cutting compound and then finish with T-Cut or similar very mild paint abrasive.

Now fit the aluminium flange formers. The flange formers and their support struts are fixed to the plug with duct (duck) tape so that the plug isn't damaged by screws.

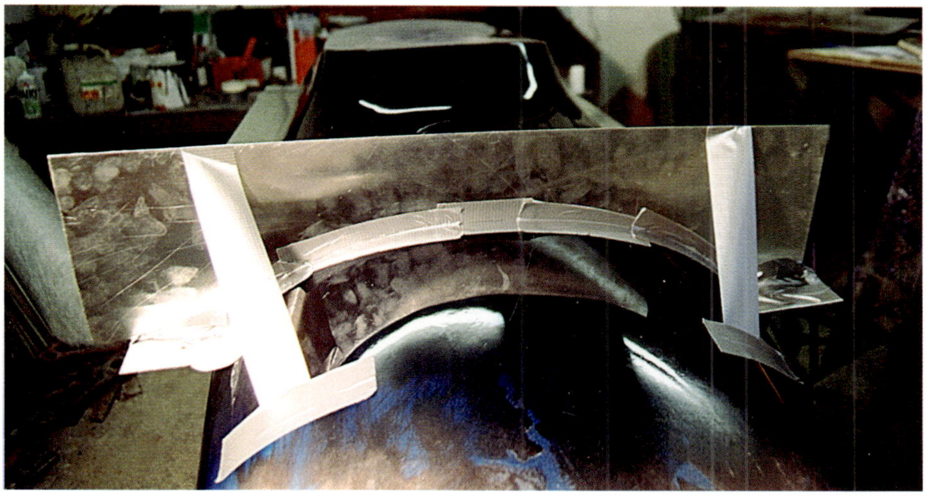

The racer's nose will be a separate component so, here, a vertical flange former has been fitted in exactly the same way as the horizontal flange fomers.

Plasticine can be used to fill the joint between the plug and flange formers (it can be mixed with mould wax to soften it, making it easier to apply) ...

... use a plastic spreader to smooth the Plasticine into the gaps.

Wax the plug (and flange formers) with five applications of mould release wax (leaving them to dry between coats before polishing with mutton cloth). Then apply the plastic release agent (PVA) with a thin sponge as pictured.

Once the PVA is dry, apply the gel coat. Leave the first gel coat to dry before applying the second. Once the second gel coat is dry (sticky), apply the GRP. Here, the grey gel coat is on the left with the first layer of glass being rollered on with a paddle roller. For moulds you'll need four or five layers of GRP.

Once all the layers of GRP have been applied and left to dry for at least two days, as shown here, remove the flange formers and then clean the plug where they were fixed. Then, after adding any new flange formers, wax and polish the area of the plug you'll be using next.

Adding more flange formers for the racer's nose cone.

Here, after polishing and release agent application, gel coats have been applied to the nose cone area of the racer plug.

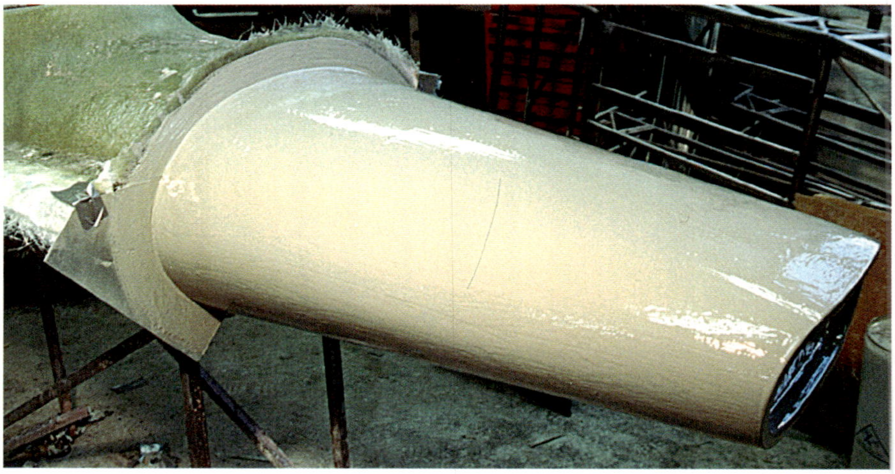

This view from the underside of the racer shows the nose cone and upper body flanges, The sill section of the plug and the new GRP flanges are waiting to go through the stages of finishing, waxing, release agent, gel coat and GRP.

The lower nose cone/sill (rocker) flange former being removed.

Right & far right: All the GRP of the upper body and nose cone moulds has now been laid (including the flanges) and has hardened. Here excess material is being cut from the GRP flanges with a power saw. If all your mould panels were now finished, you'd drill a series of holes through the cleaned up flanges, before removing the moulds from the plug so that they can be bolted together again in exactly the same relative positions. However, in this instance, we wanted to create mating flanges (using the fibreglass flanges of the already moulded mould panels) for sill (rocker) panel moulds, so we left the flanges undrilled at this point.

Removal of the finished sill (rocker) panel mould.

Steve removing the top section of the finished mould set from the plug, which leaves ...

... only the nose cone mould to be removed.

All moulds will need smoothing in the same manner as the plug: wet flatting, paint cutting compound, T-Cut (or similar mild paint abrasive) and release wax.

Because of the shape of the English Racing Automiles single-seater, access to many parts of the car, like pedals and radiator, requires that all major body panels are removable. All the moulds we've made from the plug would fit together and replicate the exact shape of the whole plug. However, in this instance, we don't want this, as we want to make flange formers on the moulds to create internal flanges in the body panels. The flanges are made by laying gel coat and GRP onto a flat, shiny surface (glass is fine) to produce sheets of flat GRP ...

... which can be used to make the flange formers as shown here.

The internal flange formers are bolted to the mould's external flanges, so holes must be drilled through both.

Newly moulded top body panel from a racing single-seater being carefully trimmed to a guideline with a saw.

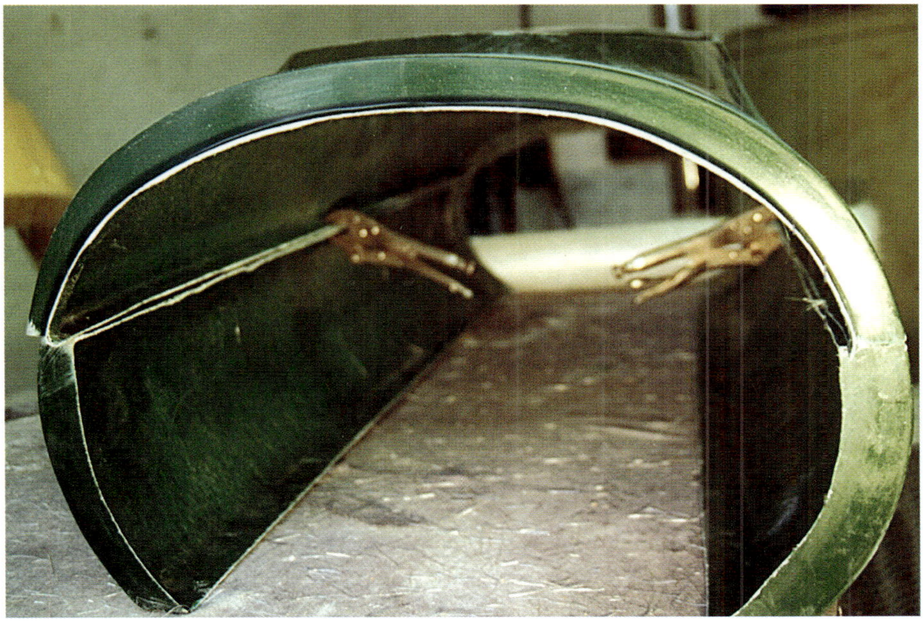

Finished moulded panels complete with internal flanges.

Single-seater racer body panels loosely assembled.

The finished racecars at Goodwood.

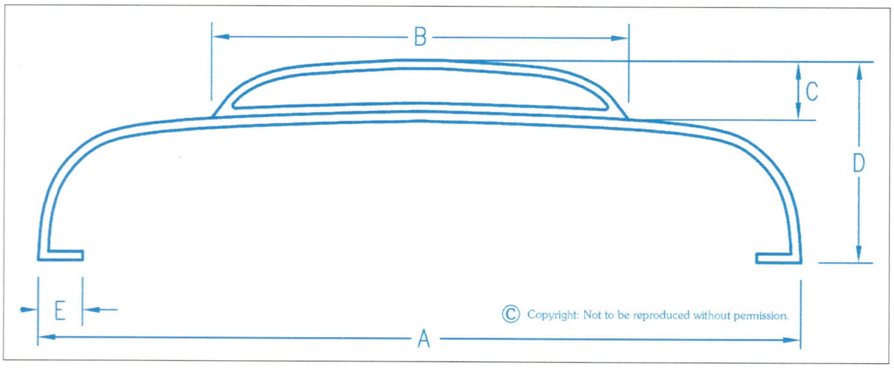

MAKING STANDARD TIGER AVON GRP BODY PANELS

The accompanying line drawings are intended as a guide to making standard GRP bodywork to fit a standard factory specification chassis. **Important!** When making new plugs to mould panels which will be fitted to a chassis and suspension system you've built yourself, **always** check actual chassis dimensions and, if necessary, adjust panel dimensions accordingly. Bear in mind, too, that individual panels will probably need to interconnect with adjacent panels and be able to fit over the finished chassis.

PAINTING GRP BODYWORK

Instead of relying on the gel coat for an attractive finish, you can paint the GRP panels. Although coloured gel coat panels can be polished to a fine finish and, if maintained and regularly polished, will keep their colour fairly well, painting the panels will give you more variety of colour choice and generally a more colourfast pigment.

There are various paint primers which are good for GRP and our paintshop has used most types successfully. Providing that the GRP was thoroughly prepared with the correct grades of abrasive papers the primers will be fine: use a coarse grade (80-120 grit) of abrasive paper first for any filler repairs to surface imperfections, then work down progressively to around 400 grade.

Next apply at least two coats of primer, rub down the primer with wet and dry 600 grade, or finer.

Drg 3.2 – Tiger Avon bonnet front view.
A = 710mm (27.95in). B = 470mm (18.5in).
C = 65mm (2.55in). D = 200mm (7.87in).
E = 20mm (0.78in).

Paul flatting a Super Six rear wing in preparation for primer and then top coats of paint.

Warning! Remember to make sure the area where you're spraying is very well ventilated and that you use the correct mask.

The application method for the final coats of paint will depend on the paint being used, so follow the manufacturer's instructions supplied with the paint.

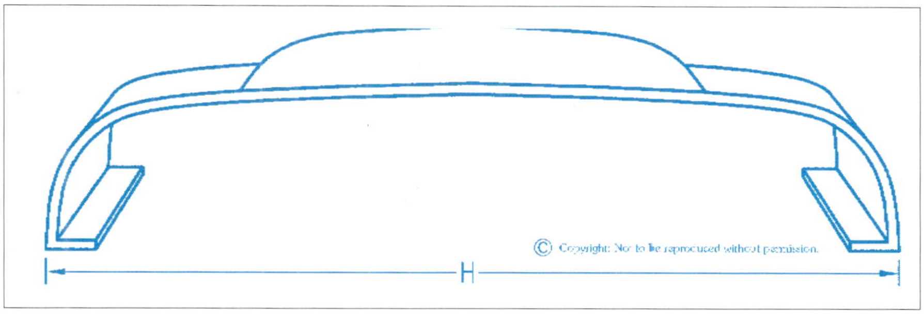

Drg 3.3 – Tiger Avon bonnet (hood) rear view. H = 940mm (37.00in).

Right, middle: Side view of Tiger Avon bonnet (hood) moulding.

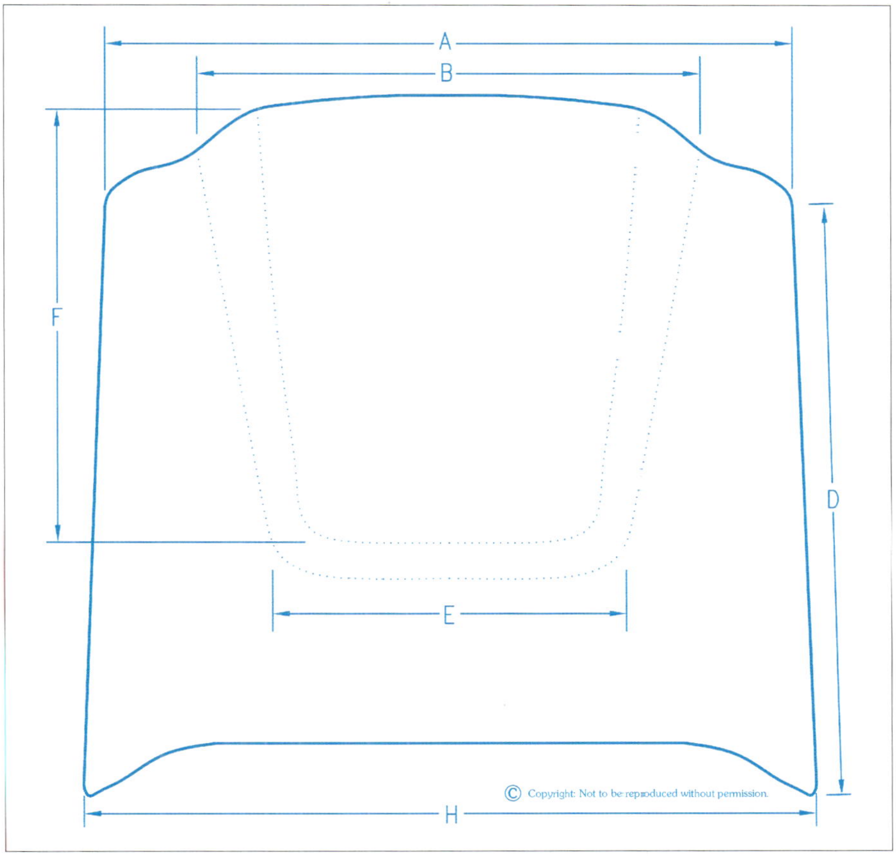

Drg 3.4.- Tiger Avon bonnet (hood) top view.
A = 710mm (27.95in). B = 470mm (18.5in). D = 925mm (36.41in). E = 400mm (15.74in). F = 660mm (25.98in). H = 940mm (37.00in).

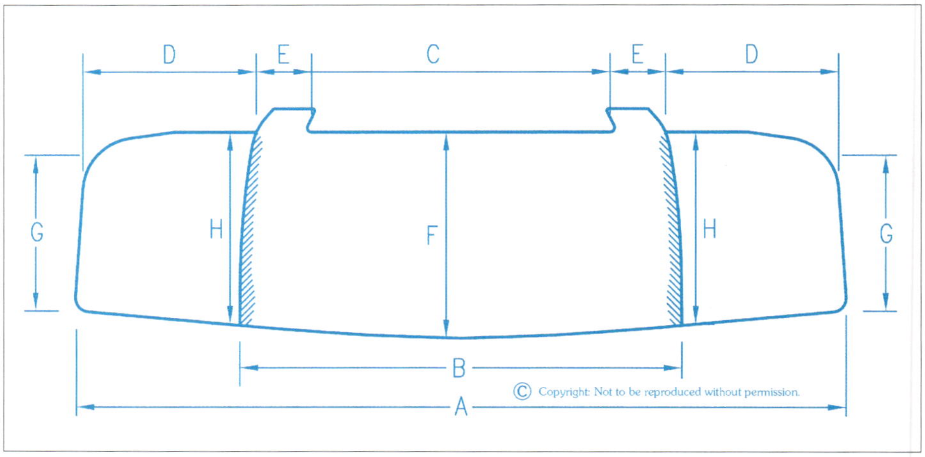

Drg 3.5 – Tiger Avon main body rear view.
A = 1685mm (66.33in). B = 1020mm (40.15in). C = 720mm (28.34in). D = 335mm (13.18in). E = 150mm (5.90in). F = 455mm (17.91in). G [centre of curve] = 395mm (15.55in). H = 440mm (17.32in).

Rear view of Tiger Avon main body moulding.

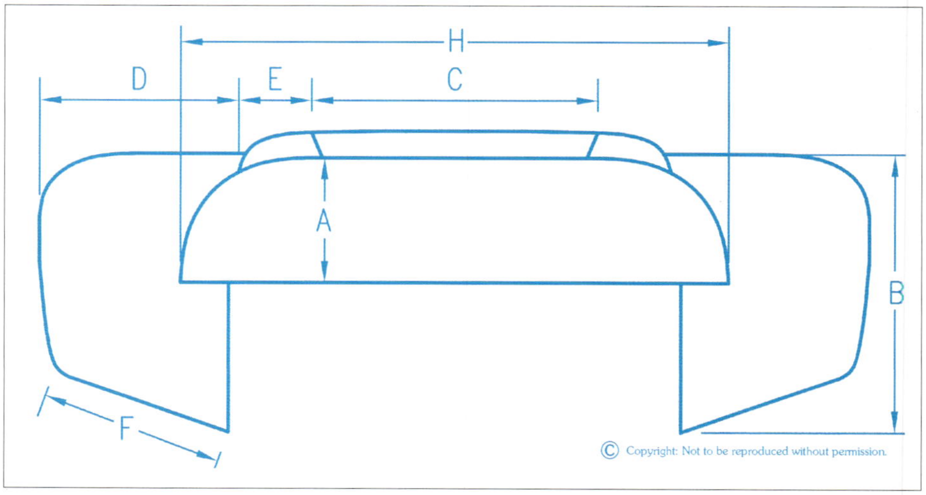

Drg 3.6 – Tiger Avon main body front view.
A = 260mm (10.23in). B = 530mm (20.86in). C = 720mm (28.34in). D = 335mm (13.18in). E = 150mm (5.90in). F = 345mm (13.58in). H = 930mm (36.61in).

Front view of Tiger Avon main body moulding.

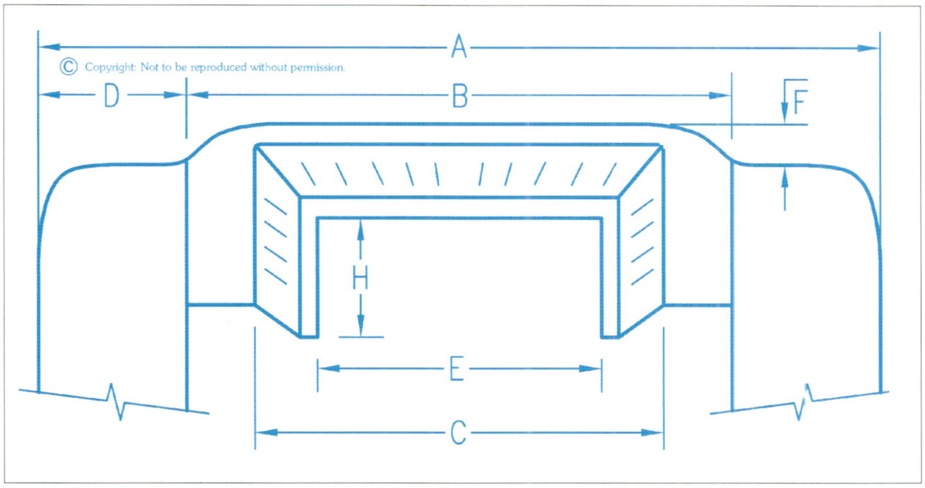

Drg 3.7 Tiger Avon rear wing (fender)/ boot (trunk) area overhead view. A = 1685mm (66.33in). B = 1020mm (40.15in). C = 720mm (28.34in). D = 340mm (13.38in). E = 620mm (24.40in). F = 100mm (3.93in). H = 265mm (10.43in).

Side and interior view of Tiger Avon main body moulding.

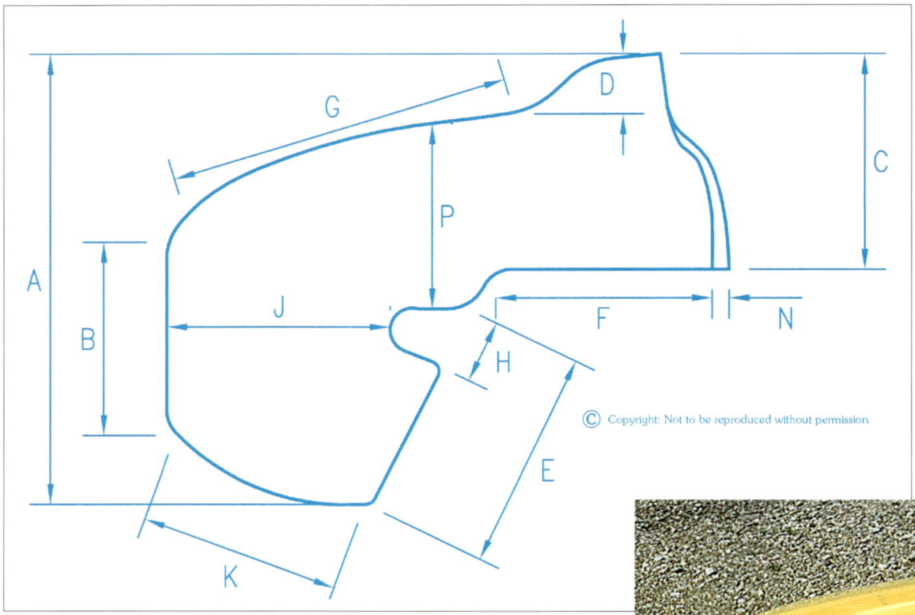

Drg 3.8 Tiger Avon nose side view.
A = 520mm (20.47in). B = 235mm (9.25in).
C = 200mm (7.87in). D = 65mm (2.55in).
E = 300mm (11.81in). F = 150mm (5.90in).
G = 440mm (17.32in). H = 60mm (2.36in).
J = 310mm (12.20in). K = 270mm (10.62in).
N = 35mm (1.37in). P = 160mm (6.29in).

Side view of Tiger Avon nose moulding.

Cycle-type wing moulding for Tiger Avon.

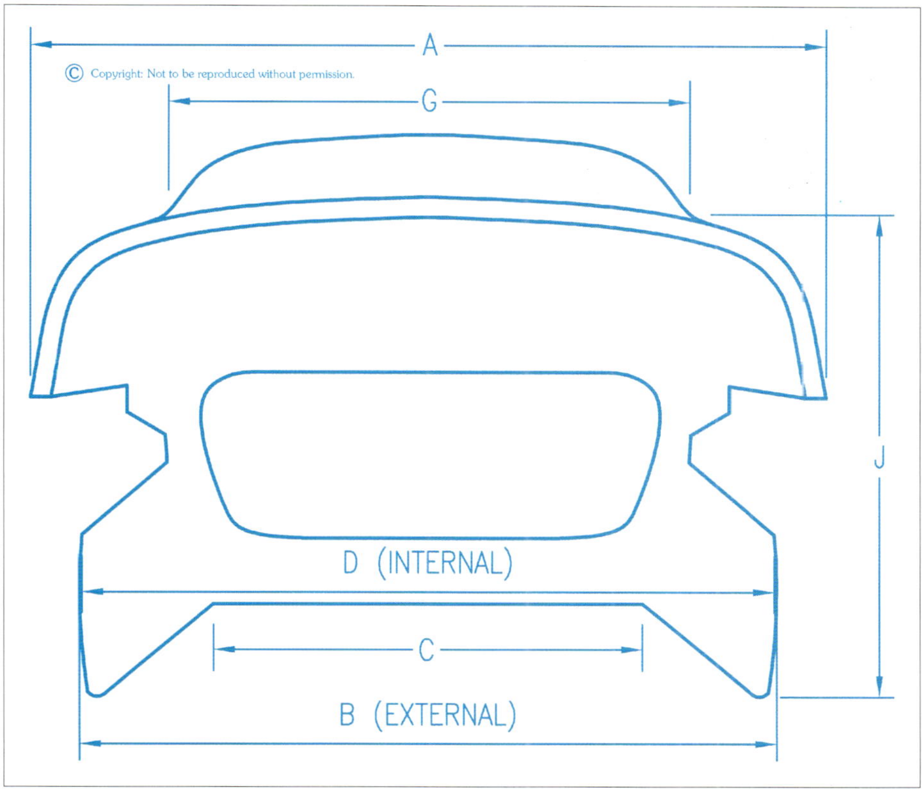

Drg 3.9 Tiger Avon nose internal view. A = 700mm (27.55in). B = 620mm (24.40in). C = 535mm (21.06in). D = 630mm (24.80in). G = 470mm (18.50in). J = 475mm (18.70in).

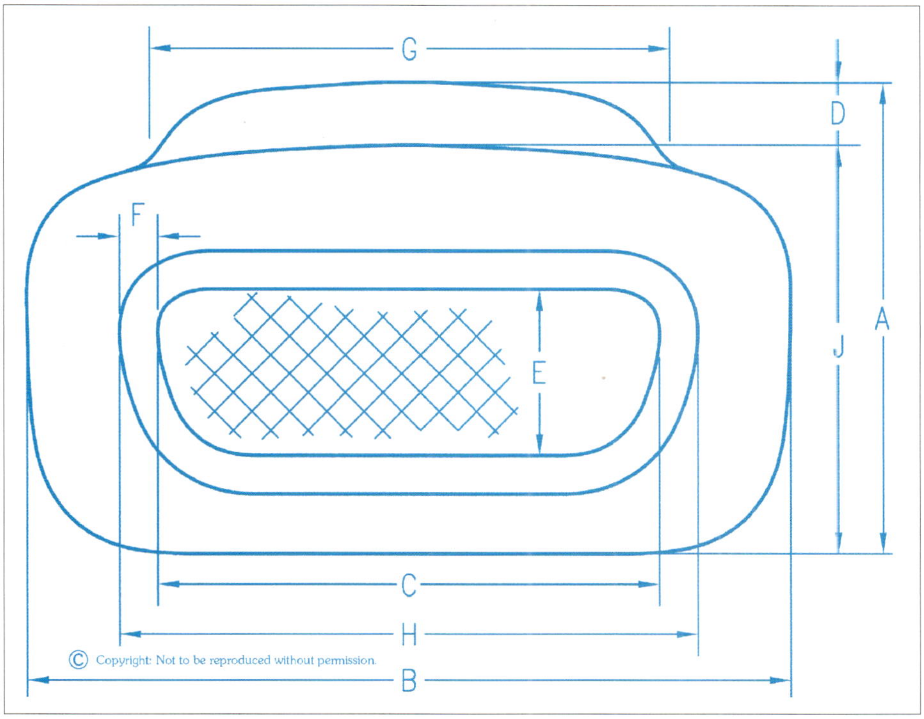

Drg 3.10 Tiger Avon nose front view. A = 520mm (20.47in). B = 560mm (22.04in). C = 435mm (17.12in). D = 65mm (2.55in). E = 180mm (7.08in). F = 25mm (0.98in). G = 470mm (18.50in). H = 520mm (20.47in). J = 455mm (17.91in)

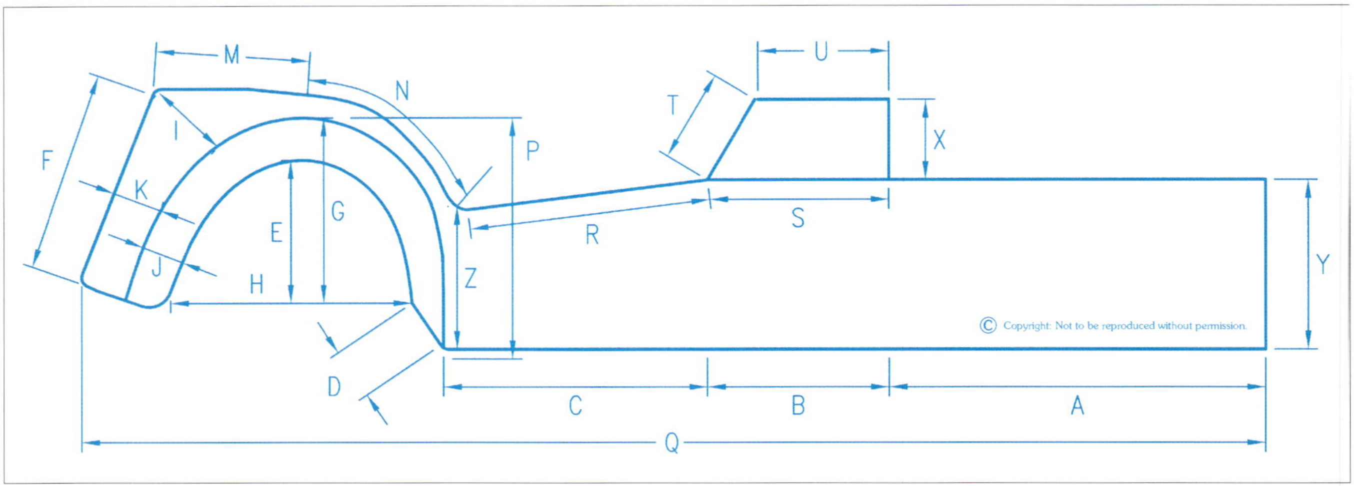

Drg 3.11 Tiger Avon main body side view.
A = 870mm (34.25in). B = 385mm (15.15in). C = 475mm (18.70in). D = 345mm (13.58in). E = 320mm (12.59in). F = 455mm (17.91in). G = 395mm (15.55in). H = 670mm (26.37in). I = 140mm (5.51in). J = 60mm (2.36in). K = 80mm (3.14in). M = 365mm (14.37in). N = 525mm (20.66in). P = 530mm (20.86in). Q = 2520mm (99.21in). R = 450mm (17.71in). S = 385mm (15.15in). T = 250mm (9.84in). U = 315mm (12.40in). X = 225mm (8.85in). Y = 350mm (13.77in). Z = 275mm (10.82in).

Side view of Tiger Avon main body moulding.

Complete set of Tiger Avon body mouldings.

Chapter 4
Interior

SEATS

The standard seats are of the 'pad'-type, which consist of four pads (two seat backs and two seat bottoms). These pad-type seats are reasonably easy to make and can look remarkably good for the relatively low cost of making them. You can use vinyl material or leather to cover the seats. It's important to note that, if you're making basic pad-type seats, or indeed a special design shape of your own, all seats from IVA (2010) must have a headrest. If using a fixed nonadjustable seat, a headrest can be attached to the top chassis rail; the minimum size and height of the headrest can be found in the IVA manual. You should find plenty of headrests in amazing condition at your local car breakers, and small, easily-fabricated brackets will hold these to the rear of your seats. Alternatively, aftermarket seats are available from Tiger supplied with the tiger logo.

Equipment required

Sewing machine (industrial)
Staple gun
Craft knife

Materials required

Vinyl material or leather
Plywood board
Sponge
Strong cotton or thread (36M)

Finished pad seat bases.

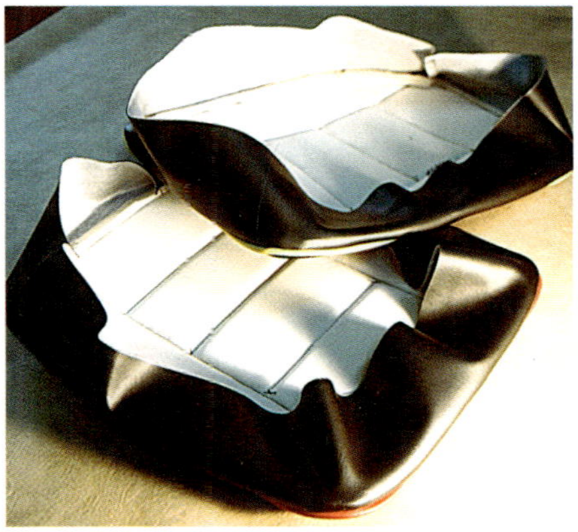

Vinyl seat covers ready to be fitted over foam pads.

String (3-4mm/0.12-0.16in)
Glue (impact adhesive type)

The first job is to decide the size and shape of the pad seats you're going to make. Are the corners going to be round or square? What thickness of sponge is required? Remember, if you're a tall driver then maybe you'll need thinner back pads to give yourself more legroom: the reverse may be true if you're not so tall. As a guide, the standard base and back pads on most Tigers are usually 50mm (2in) thick, to allow for taller drivers.

To make the piping to stitch around the seat edges, use a piece of thick string to create the round shape. Cut a piece of vinyl or leather approximately 50mm (2in) wide fold it over the string and then stitch the vinyl/ leather close to the string. Alternatively, you can purchase lengths of piping in different colours.

The gusset of vinyl or leather covering the sides of the seat base or seatback will need to be approximately twice the depth of the sponge to allow for stitching and leave enough material to fix to the seat base/back.

The material for the seat surface or backrest face will be approximately the same size as the sponge pad. To give a padded effect to the seating area it's possible to stick a thin (approximately 3mm/0.12in thick) layer of sponge to the back of the vinyl and then stitch your pattern through the vinyl and sponge padding layer.

The sponge seat base and backrest cushions will be approximately 12.7mm (0.5in) larger all around than the plywood base/backboard.

The seat material is sewn from the inside, so for each pad start by sewing together the pieces of the gusset, then sew the completed gusset to the seat cover using piping at the joint.

Stick the sponge to the plywood base (it should overlap the wood by 12.7mm/0.5in on all sides).

Turn the cover from inside out and pull it over the sponge seat base or backrest cushion and then turn the whole thing upside-down. Apply suitable impact adhesive to the periphery of the plywood base or backboard and the overlapping material. Then, starting with the corners, pull the vinyl tight enough to compress the edges of the sponge and stick it to the base. Finish the fixing by using a staple gun to secure the material to the base/backboard.

If you're going to attempt to make seats with a more complex shape – and possibly adjustable – then you're

A set of pad seats in an early Tiger Cub.

With the change from SVA (Single Vehicle Approval) to the current IVA (Individual Vehicle Approval) test, seats like these no longer meet the criteria. In this instance, headrests can be made and bolted to the top chassis rail. It's important not only to check requirements on size of the headrest, but also the height and indeed gap (if any) between seat and headrest.

An example of a high-back seat: this type of seat or individual headrest is required for IVA.

Handbrake (parking brake) area detail of a carbon fibre transmission tunnel installed in a car.

advised to buy GRP seat shells which you can trim: such shells are available at very reasonable prices. Another way is to fabricate the seat frame in steel tube.

HANDBRAKE & GEARSTICK GAITERS

The handbrake and gearstick gaiters can be made from the same vinyl material or leather as the seat covers. As with the seat covers, stitch these inside out when making them.

CARPET

Most builders carpet their Tigers.

You can purchase the carpet in two ways. First, there are various companies that sell car-type carpet by the roll or metre (you can find them in various magazines). Second, you can buy a ready trimmed set from Tiger.

If you want to make your own carpets, after cutting them to shape you can trim the edges with vinyl. First cut off a strip of the vinyl material approximately 38mm (1.5in) wide and as long as the edge of the carpet you're going to trim.

Fold over one edge of the vinyl by about 8mm (0.3in) and stitch the fold for the length of the strip; repeat the procedure the other side of the strip to give two neat edges.

Now fold the vinyl around the

Tiger R6 carbon fibre transmission tunnel.

edge of the carpet and stitch through vinyl and carpet to give a really neat vinyl edging to the carpet.

ALUMINIUM TRIM

You can give a nice finish to the interior of your Tiger by finishing off with aluminium, rather like most racers. However, remember the aluminium will tend to discolour if it gets damp, so you'll have to keep on top of the problem by regular polishing with wax to seal the surface. **Warning!** No sharp edges are allowed for IVA (check the IVA manual).

CARBON FIBRE TRIM

Another, but more expensive way, of trimming the interior of your Tiger is with carbon fibre panels. You can purchase sheets of flat carbon fibre to trim things like the interior side panels and behind the seats; the transmission tunnel can also be made in carbon fibre (see illustrations which show Tiger R6 tunnels).

The dashpanel can be made in carbon fibre or aluminium. **Warning!** Remember that there is an IVA

Top: Early Tiger Super Six with what would otherwise be non-compliant gauges recessed sufficiently in the dashpanel (fascia) to pass the IVA test.

Middle: Late Tiger Cat (lhd) with recessed instruments and with radiused lower edge to dashpanel (fascia).

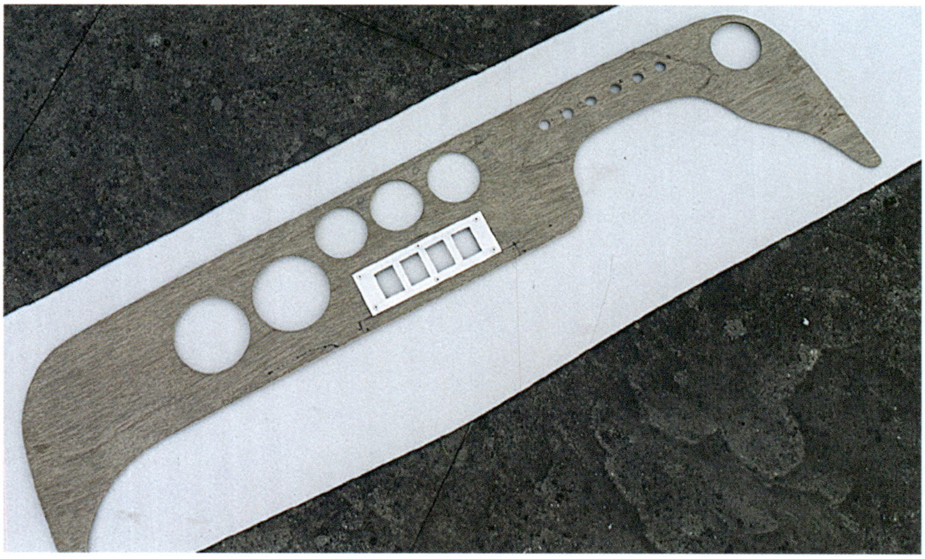

A plywood dashpanel (fascia) about to be covered with vinyl material.

Most builders will use fabric stuck over a shaped aluminium or plywood sheet to create the dashpanel for their Tiger Avon. The first step is to clamp the pre-shaped panel to the fibreglass dashpanel and then, having carefully planned the layout, cut the instrument, switch and warning (idiot) light openings through both simultaneously.

Check fit all the instruments and switches before unclamping the aluminium or plywood sheet which will become the dashpanel.

This dashpanel has already had the openings for instruments and swiches cut before it was covered with fabric. The panel is now glued to the fibreglass dashpanel before holes are carefully cut in the fabric to allow the instrument, switch and warning (idiot) light bodies to be pushed through.

IVA-compliant recessed horn button on a Super Six.

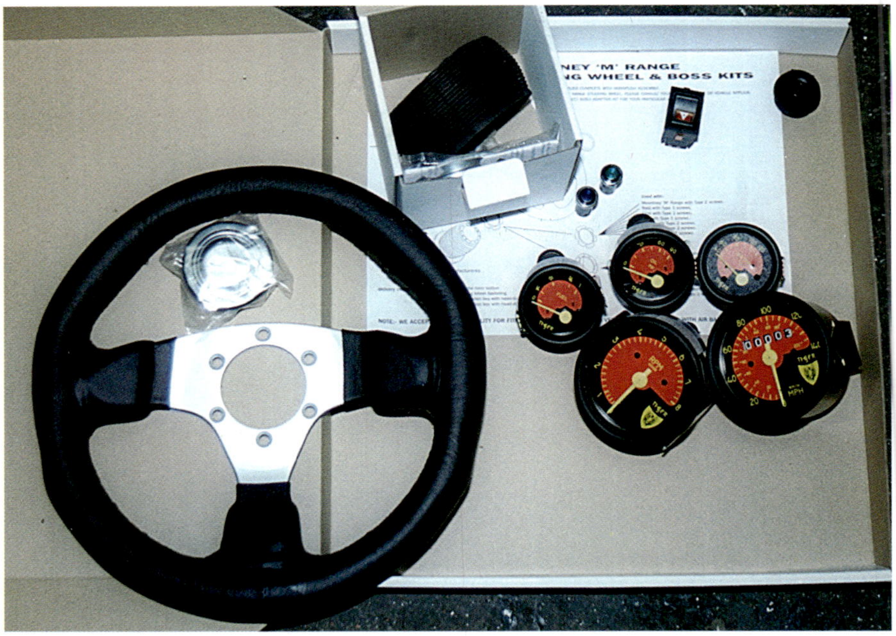

Gauges, steering wheel and boss (all IVA-compliant).

requirement for the bottom of the dash to be radiused, so check this out in the IVA regulations.

DASHBOARD (FASCIA/ INSTRUMENT PANEL)

The dash can be made in various ways, but will have to be IVA compliant in the UK (**Warning!** It should have no sharp or unradiused edges). The accompanying photographs show a number of dashboard designs and solutions to IVA compliance problems.

If your car design is more adventurous, say, rather like the Tiger Storm, then you may be thinking of a mould with much more shape to it for the dash. However, remember the radius required on the edges for IVA, especially on the lower edge. Check the IVA manual if in doubt.

Laura checking a Tiger Storm dashpanel for good fit around the trim edge at front. This design shows just how imaginative you can be when it comes to dashboard design, though the traditional 'flat dash' probably best suits Clubman-type cars like the Avon.

Chapter 5
Motorcycle engines

Kawasaki ZX9R engine/gearbox installation in a Tiger B6. The Avon chassis will require some fairly simple adaptation to house a motorcycle engine.

There are quite a lot of advantages to be had by fitting a bike engine instead or a car unit: they're generally very powerful for their capacity and physical size, and rev higher and generally weigh a lot less than a conventional car engine with similar power. The sequential 6-speed gearbox associated with most motorcycle engines is also very light.

Power to weight ratio is the key factor.

The Tiger B6 (Bike 6) weighs in at around 460kgs (1013lb) with its 900cc Kawasaki bike engine. Of course, sports bikes don't have reverse gears. However, reverse boxes (which are installed in the driveline between the bike gearbox and rear axle) are now available and the B6 is so equipped.

The Tiger Avon chassis will require some modifications if a bike engine is to be used.

The accompanying photos

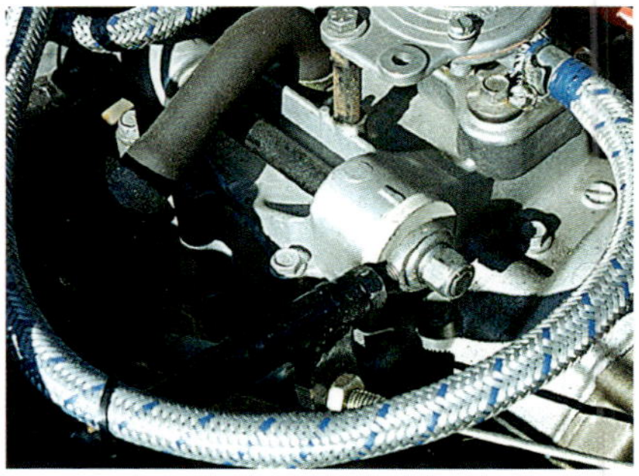

A Kawasaki ZX9R engine before installation.

Top right: Tiger B6 Kawasaki 900cc engine showing Rose-jointed stabiliser/support arms.

Bottom, right: Lower engine/gearbox mounting on a B6 chassis. Note that bike engine installations can be bolted direct to the chassis (no rubber mountings) as shown here.

Right & top of following page: Two views of a Kawasaki 1200cc engine in a Tiger B6.

show detail of motorcycle engines in Tiger chassis.

There are various ways to install a motorcycle engine and gearbox, but generally the engine and gearbox will be bolted direct to the chassis.

As mentioned earlier, the bike gearbox will be a sequential unit, but will not have a reverse gear which is a major disadvantage for a car.

In all installations a driveline from the bike gearbox to the car's rear axle

A typical central propshaft bearing.

A simple forward/reverse secondary gearbox with two drive flanges for two short propshafts (driveshafts).

A short propshaft (driveshaft) for use with a forward/reverse secondary gearbox.

differential will be required. First the bike gearbox will have to have its chain sprocket removed and a new drive flange fitted in its place.

The engine/gearbox unit will be mounted in the car so that its drive flange faces to the rear of the car. **Caution!** A direct drive system (gearbox flange to diff flange) with no reverse box would normally require a long propshaft and this is **not recommended** due to loads it will

A forward/reverse gearbox mounted in the transmission tunnel. Note the forward/reverse lever and linkage. The bracket across the tunnel takes the gearchange lever which will operate the primary gearbox via a push-pull cable system. Both levers will protrude through purpose-made holes with trimmed edges in the transmission tunnel.

This small alloy radiator in a Tiger B6 was taken from a small Japanese hatchback. A standard Tiger radiator could also be used.

impart to the new output drive flange of the bike gearbox. So, if you're not going to install a reverse box, make sure you split the propshaft with a central bearing (rather like the central bearing on the Ford Sierra propshaft).

Note that if you're building a Tiger to race in the 750 Motor Club race series, it should have a means of reversing under its own power, but check the regulations with the motor club.

If you're going to fit a reverse box in the central tunnel area, you'll need two short propshafts (see accompanying picture). **Caution!** When having your

Two 1000cc (injected) Suzuki motorcycle engines in the Tiger Z100 Mark 2.

propshafts made, make sure they're balanced for high speeds.

A gearchange mechanism for the sequential bike box can be made using a Rose-jointed linkage from a centrally-mounted lever, or a push and pull cable system can be used instead.

The lower mounts of the motorcycle engine/gearbox unit will bolt direct to the chassis, the upper mounts and stabiliser will need to be made up from small adjustable rods with Rose joints at each end.

The plumbing of the bike engine is similar to most 4-cylinder car engines and usually you can use the associated bike radiator. If you're doubtful about cooling capacity, you can use the radiator from a small car.

You can use the rpm gauge from the donor motorcycle, or a purpose-made 80mm instrument can be bought.

Tiger has now stopped producing its twin bike-engined car, the Z100 Mark 2. This model had two Suzuki GSXR 1000cc engines that provided drive into a special transfer box. Power to weight ratio was around 570bhp/ton, and the car reached 0-60mph in close to 3 seconds (faster than the Maclaren F1 sports car)! Even more extreme is the Tiger Z100WR: a 4wd Z100 with two 1200cc Kawasaki engines which has been timed at 2.8sec 0-60mph and 6.3sec 0-100mph.

It's worth noting that the IVA exhaust emissions test for most motorcycle engine fitments is very difficult to pass because the higher emission limits are not necessary when applied to a motorcycle; this is one of the reasons why Tiger has not continued to produce this model as a factory-built car.

Chapter 6
Chassis & wishbones

A few important points before you start to weld your chassis.

SAFETY & FIRST-AID

Warning! If you're working alone in your garage or workshop ask your family or friends to look in from time to time to check that you're OK and to help with heavy lifting. If working with a helper who has an accident always call an ambulance as a first priority if an injury appears to be more than minor.

Burns or scalds

To ease a scald or burn, hold the affected area under cold running water or in cold water for around 15 minutes then cover with gauze and seek medical advice.

Protection

Warning! When welding, wear welding gloves and appropriate eye protection at all times.

A thick pair of leather gloves offer good hand protection when welding or grinding.

Welders' arc eye

Warning! You can damage or injure the corneas of your eyes if you expose your naked eyes to the welding arc. Screen your welding from others' eyes and ensure your welding mask has no cracks in the filter lens.

Should you experience arc eye the symptoms, which normally occur a few hours after exposure, will feel rather like lots of grit in the eyes. The eyes will also be red and will water badly. If you have the symptoms of arc eye you're advised to seek immediate medical advice.

Ventilation

Warning! Argon gas is heavier than air and can settle at floor level if not extracted from the garage or workshop. Argon can cause asphyxiation, so make sure your work area is very well ventilated.

Table stand

When starting to build your chassis, a flat area is needed. A table stand with a flat steel surface is ideal. Use a spirit level to ensure the table top is level.

INTRODUCTION TO MIG WELDING

MIG (Metal Inert Gas) welding is also known as 'metal arc gas-shielded welding.'

Typical MIG welding machine.

First, for the general size of the tube and steel being used in the Tiger Avon a minimum of a 130amp machine is recommended. A higher amperage machine can always be set lower so, if funds allow, buy a 180 or 200amp machine. A secondhand 200amp welder may represent better value than a new 130amp unit.

Test welds

Warning! Unless you're already experienced, it's very important that you practice your welding *before* you start welding your car's chassis.

First try a butt weld with, say, two pieces of 1in square tube. Set the MIG welder to a wire speed feed of 3.5 and, if you have a flow meter for the gas supply, set this at 10 litres per minute (approximately). If your MIG welding set is a 130amp unit, initially set it at three quarters of its maximum power.

Hold the gun approximately 15mm (0.6in) away from your work. If on your first trial the MIG wire seems to be trying to weld but also tries to push the gun away from the work, try more power and, if this does seem better, also try a slightly faster wire feed setting.

Take a look at your butt weld: is it very flat? If so, maybe faster wire feed or less power will help. If the weld is too bulky, too raised from the work, try slowing the wire feed or using more power.

You'll find that the optimum settings will come with practice. As you progress to welding thicker material these settings will need to be changed: experimenting again is the only answer to finding 'the knack.'

Problems

If your welding wire snags, release the trigger on the gun immediately. Then try cleaning the tip (burnt wire) or replacing the tip. Note that the nylon wire tube can fuse to the tip – you can unscrew the gun's nozzle and pull out the inner tube to inspect it. If the tube has melted it will need replacing. All of these problems can tangle the roll of welding wire and the wire feed rollers. If this happens, you'll need to cut off the tangled wire and then re-feed the welding wire through the gun.

Check also your shielding gas feed is OK as you cannot weld with the MIG system without a shielding gas. If the

Example of a butt weld for which too much power has been used.

This weld is the result of too fast a wire speed and too little power.

gas feed is set too low the welding tip may be getting too hot.

Note, too, that strong draughts can adversely affect the gas shield.

Weld quality checking

STATUS (Specialist Transport Advisory & Testing Utility Society) is based at Manchester Metropolitan University and has many specialist car manufacturers as members. Through STATUS, the university can undertake a wide range of vehicle related tests. These include seatbelt anchorage tests, door latch and hinge tests, and tests on many other motor vehicle related parts.

STATUS has indicated that it will do approval tests on any welding samples sent to them by anyone wishing for peace of mind about the quality of their own welding. You can find their telephone number listed in an appendix.

FUEL TANK

The fuel tank can be made from steel or aluminium (the diagram on the opposite page gives dimensions).

The fuel filler (usually 2in/50mm dia) is welded on top of the fuel tank, making sure it's location complies with IVA (some racing rules will require particular positioning/specification). A flexible fuel hose connects the filler to the petrol cap neck on the rear panel (could also be on top of the rear boot area).

On manufacturing the tank, a fuel feed tube (usually 8mm dia.) will go down inside the tank, ending just short of the bottom. Around 40mm of the tube is left protruding from the top (or indeed the side) and fuel exits from this point. A venting hole is drilled in the top of the tank and

Butt weld created with right power setting but too high a wire speed.

Result of welding with far too little argon gas: note 'air-bubble' appearance.

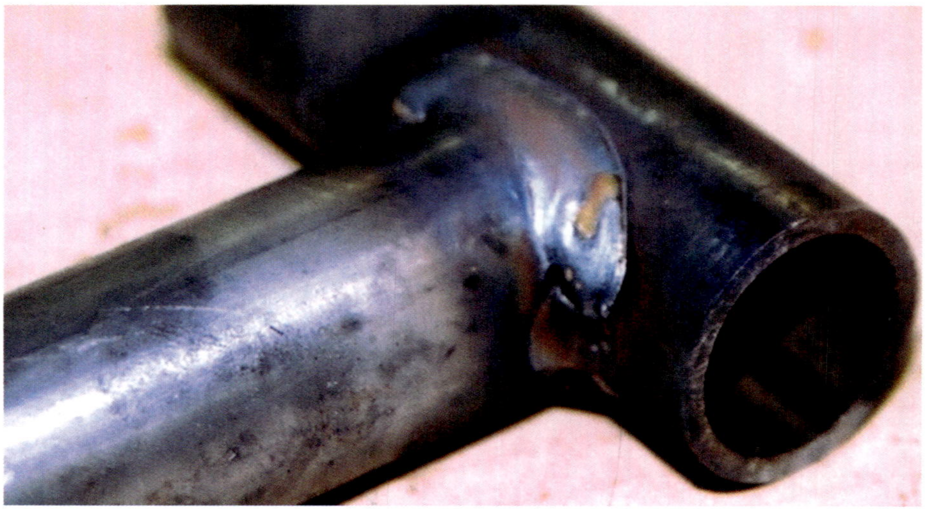

A good weld produced by the correct amount of power, correct wire speed and correct gas flow.

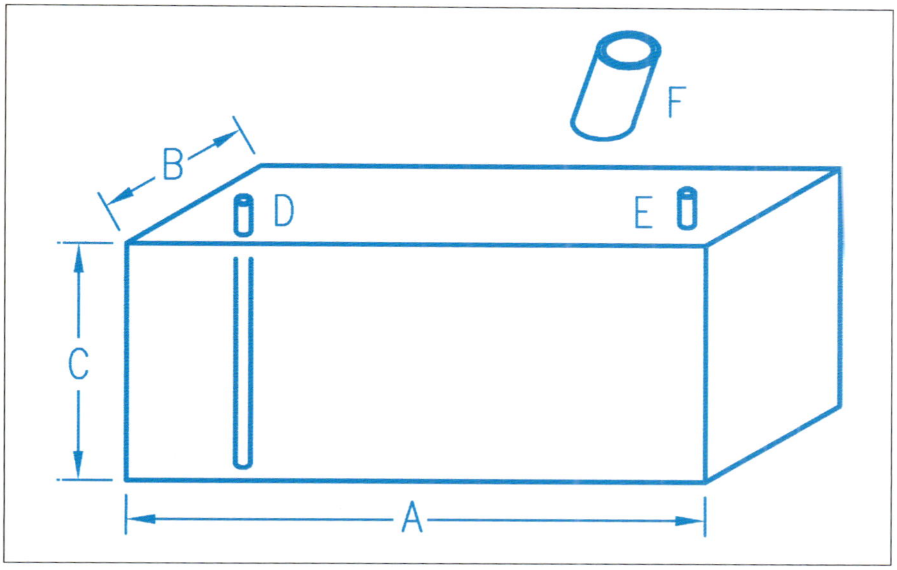

Drg 6.1 Tiger Avon fuel tank detail. A = 700mm (27.55in). B = 190mm (7.48in). C = 215mm (8.46in). D = 8mm (0.31in) outside diameter. E = 8mm (0.31in) outside diameter. F = 50mm (1.96in).

Drg 6.2 Seatbelt anchorages.

a small tube is welded to it. A rubber hose usually connects this tube to a one-way rollover valve.

Note that if your car will have fuel-injection, the tank will need to accommodate a fuel return pipe as well as a fuel feed pipe (both 8mm). Also a 'pot' of approximately 50 per cent of tank height will need to be built into the tank design: the fuel return pipe returning fuel to the tank via the pot. The pot (a small tank) will be welded inside the main fuel tank and will 'hold' fuel during hard cornering/braking/ acceleration to avoid fuel surge. A capacity of around 0.5 litre (1 pint) will usually be sufficient.

Brackets or flat bars can be welded to the underside of the tank, and these will need to be drilled to take 8mm bolts to secure the tank to both horizontal chassis tubes at the rear of the chassis.

SEATBELT ANCHORAGES

There are various ways of fixing your car's seatbelt anchorages to the chassis, but remember that all threaded fixings **must** be welded to the chassis to meet IVA requirements. It's well worthwhile checking the IVA manual for its current advice on height, width, etc.

CHASSIS & SUSPENSION WISHBONES CONSTRUCTION

The accompanying chassis and suspension drawings are for the Tiger Avon in its standard form with independent rear suspension.

Important! As individual homebuilt chassis are not built on a jig there will be small individual variations. Therefore, once your chassis is built, check all the relevant chassis dimensions against suspension drawings before making the suspension components because you may have to make some adjustments for *your* car. In particular, check chassis bracket positions and make the small adjustments required on top and bottom wishbones and hubs to fit the brackets on the chassis. When fabricating your car's rear suspension uprights (hub carriers), trial fit the driveshafts from the donor Sierra on the front faces of the hubs to ensure correct hole spacing.

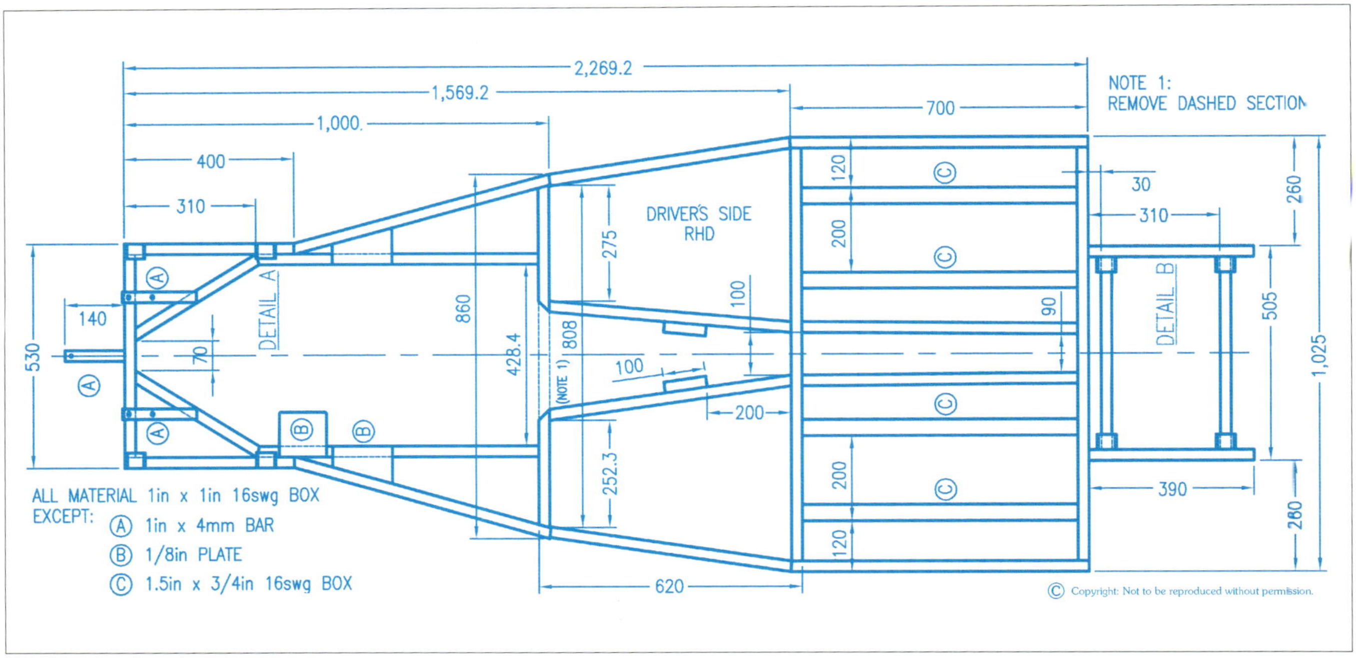

Drg 6.3a Tiger Avon lower chassis plan view (see Drg 6.3c). Dimensions in millimetres.

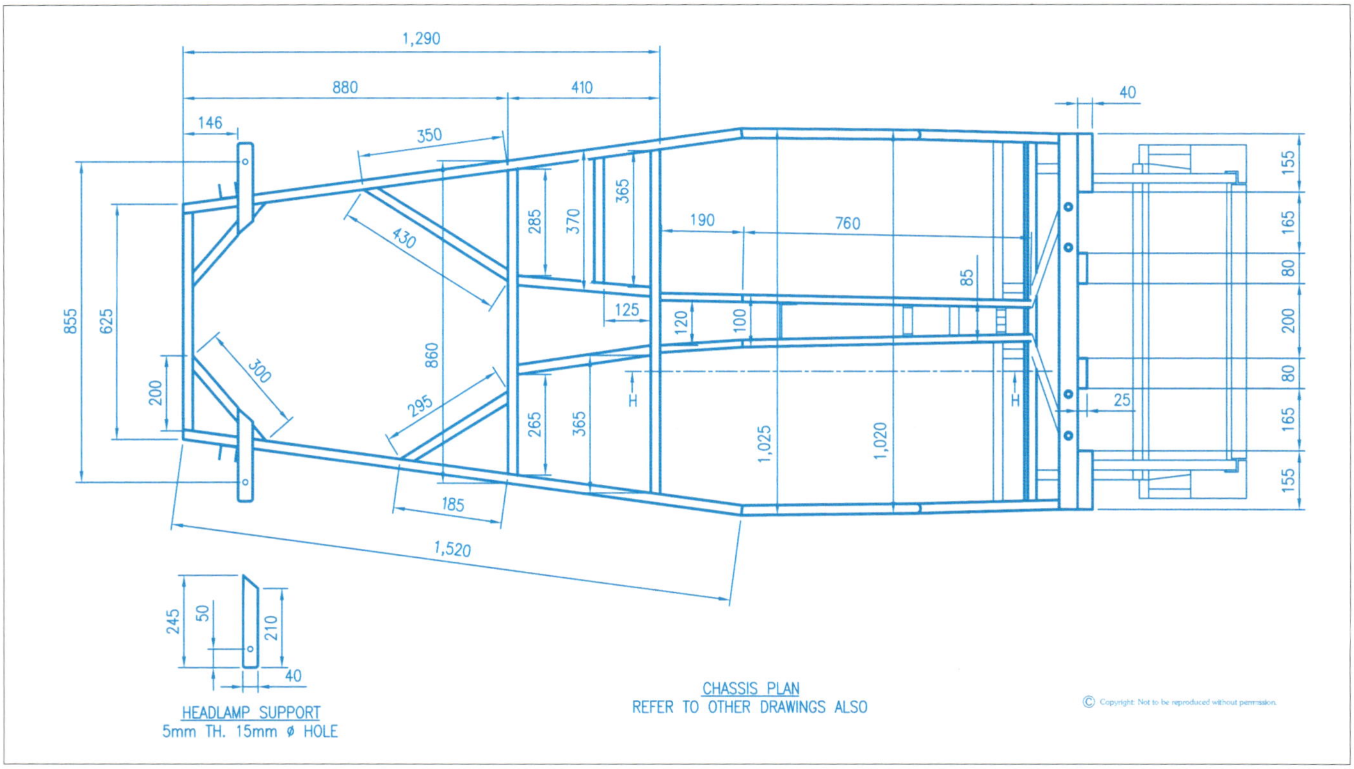

Drg 6.3b Tiger Avon upper chassis plan view. Dimensions in millimetres.

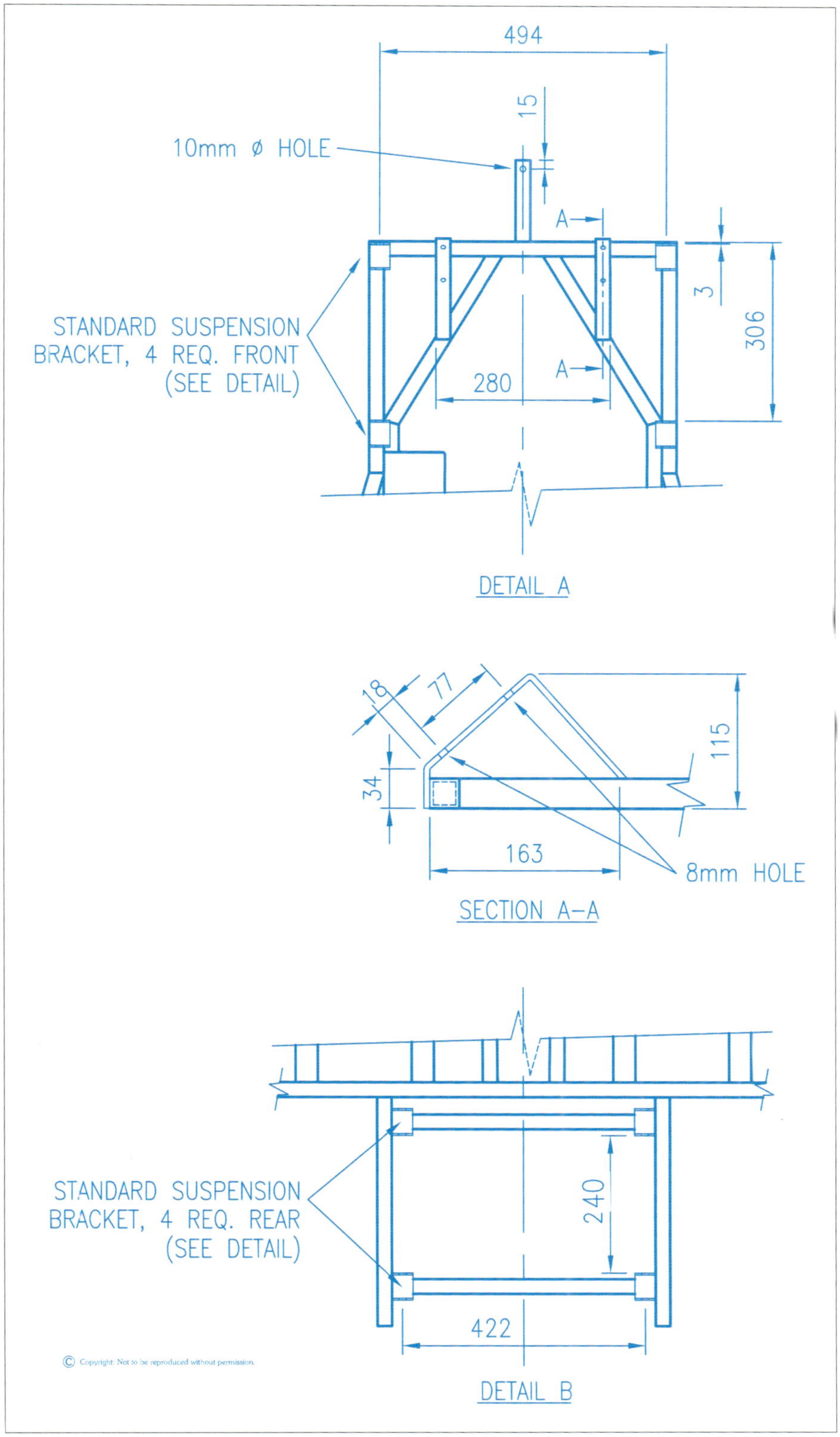

Drg 6.3c Detail of chassis area A & B (see Drg 6.3A). Dimensions in millimetres.

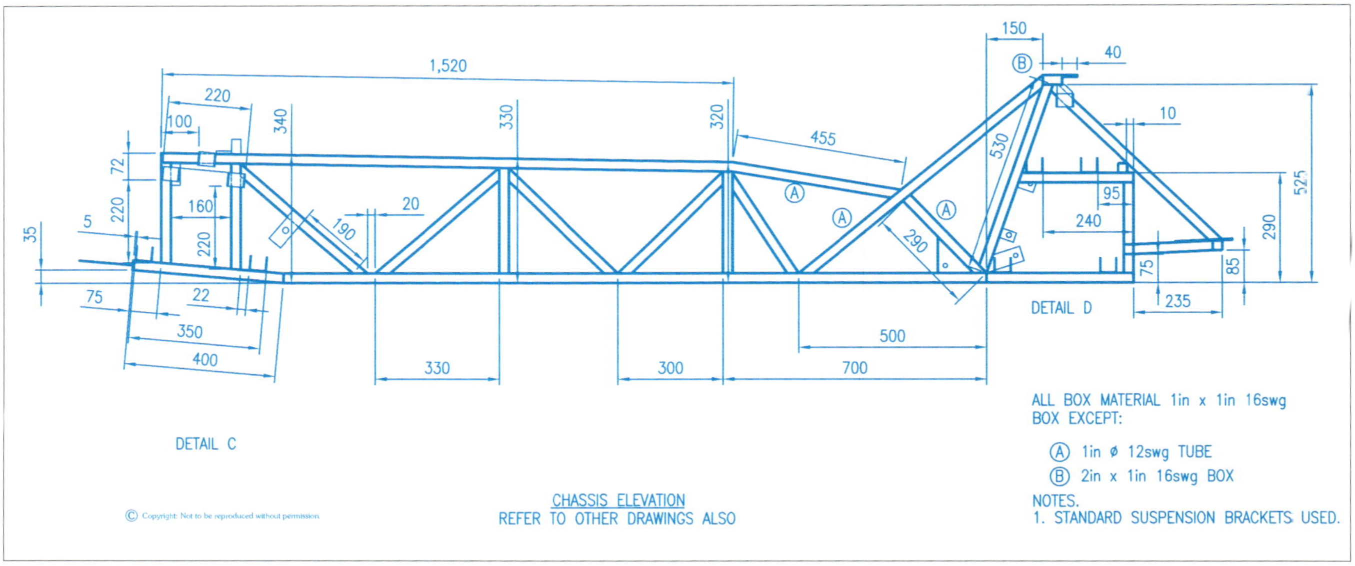

Drg 6.4 Tiger Avon chassis side elevation. Dimensions in millimetres.

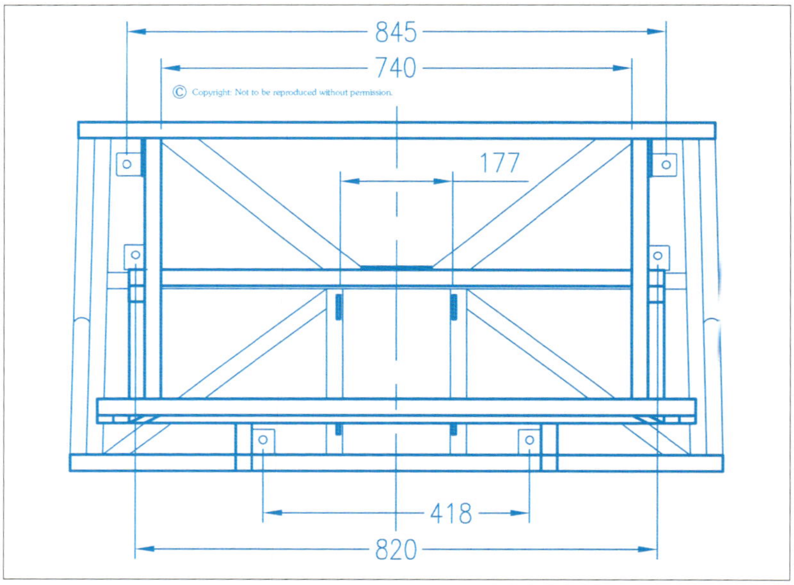

Drg 6.5 Tiger Avon chassis rear elevation. Dimensions in millimetres.

Drg 6.6 Key to Tiger Avon chassis section drawings.

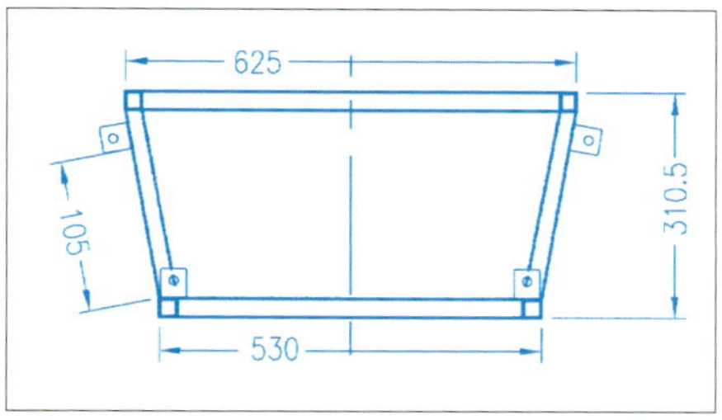

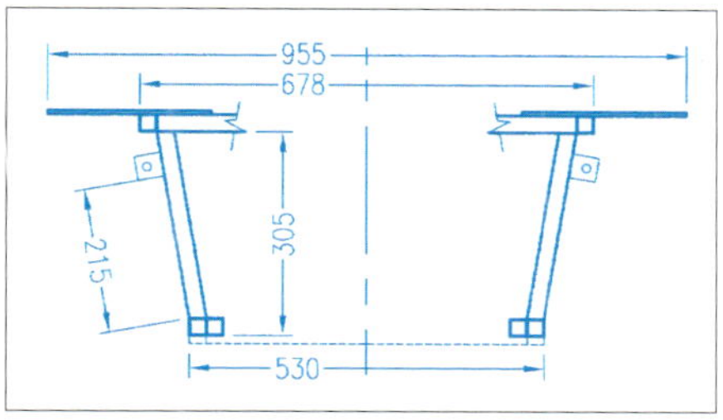

Far left: Drg 6.6a Chassis section B-B (see Drg 6.6). Dimensions in millimetres.

Drg 6.6b Chassis section C-C (see Drg 6.6). Dimensions in millimetres.

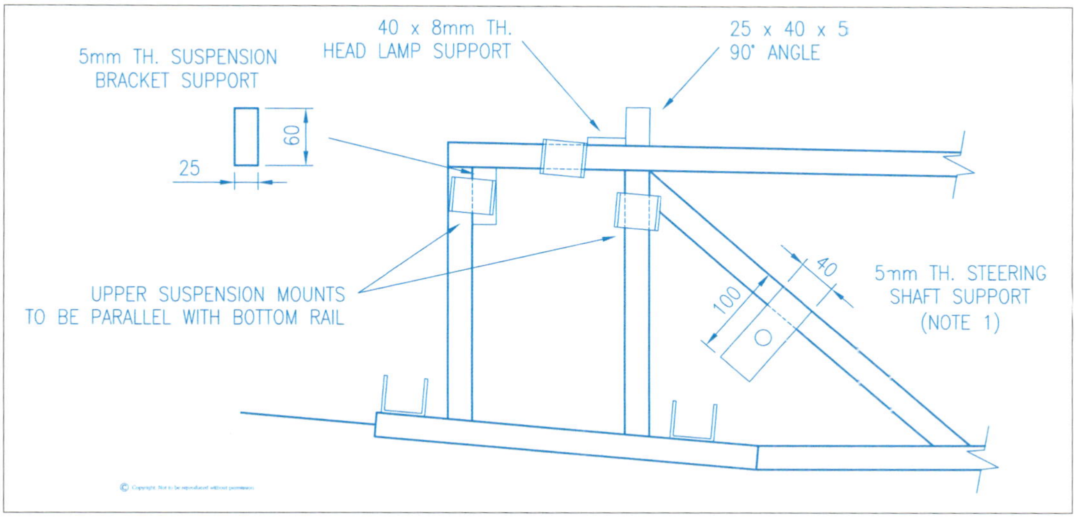

Drg 6.6c Detail of chassis area C (see Drg 6.6). Dimensions in millimetres.

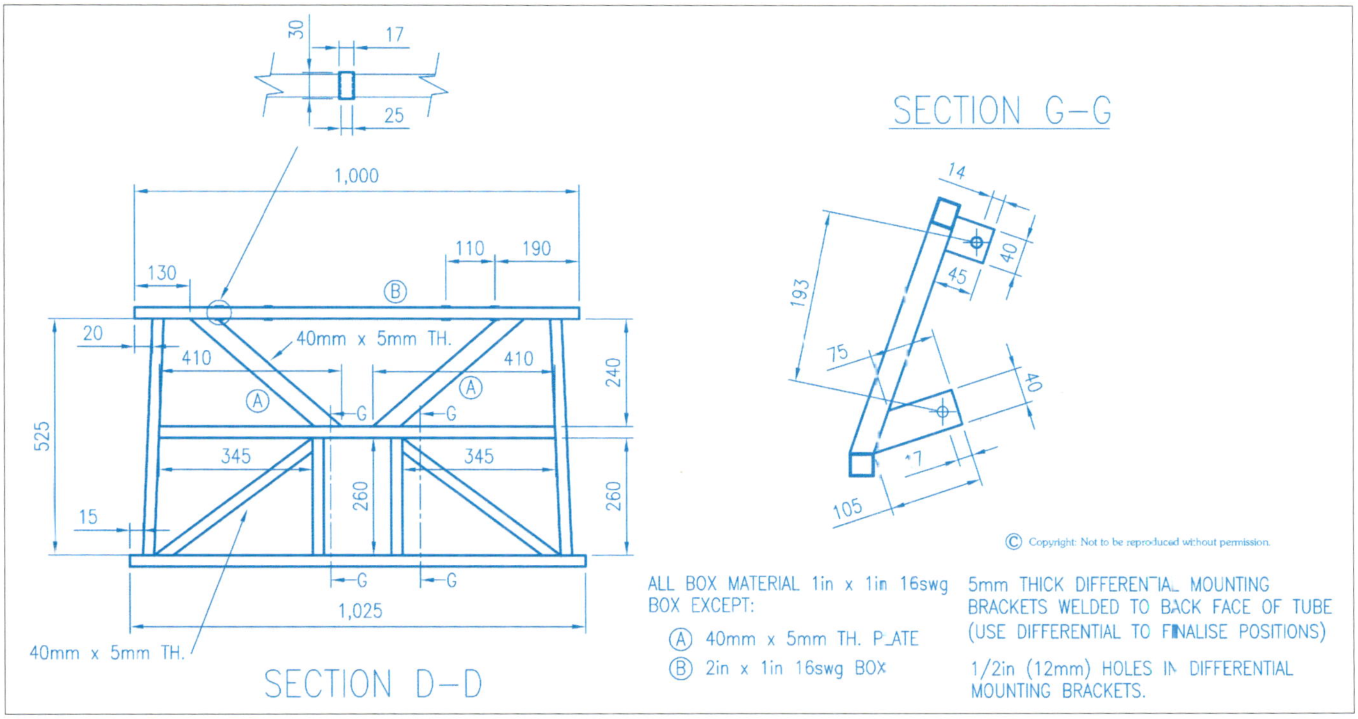

Drg 6.6d Chassis section D-D & G-G (see Drg 6.6). Dimensions in millimetres.

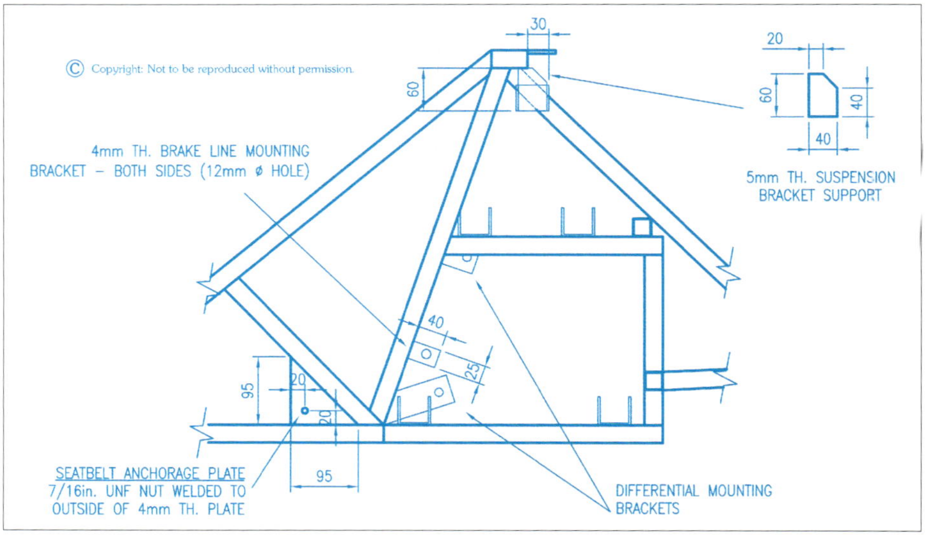

Drg 6.6e Detail of chassis area D (see Drg 6.6). Dimensions in millimetres.

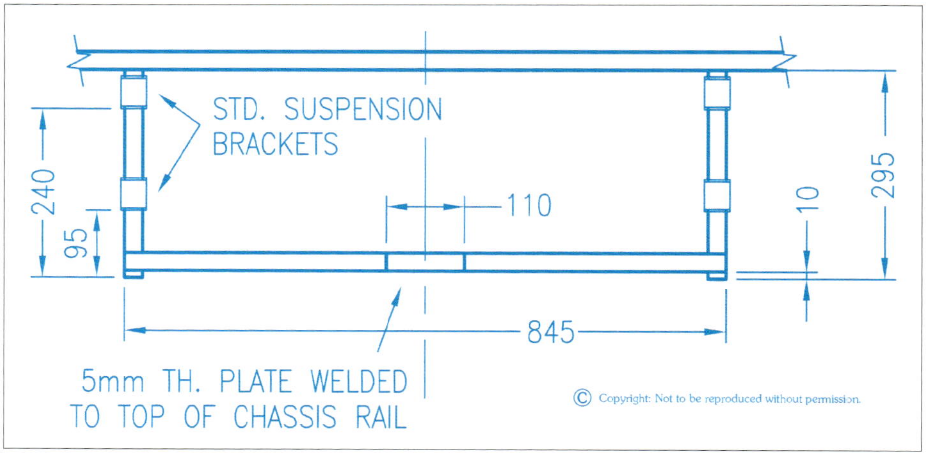

Drg 6.6f Chassis section E-E (see Drg 6.6). Dimensions in millimetres.

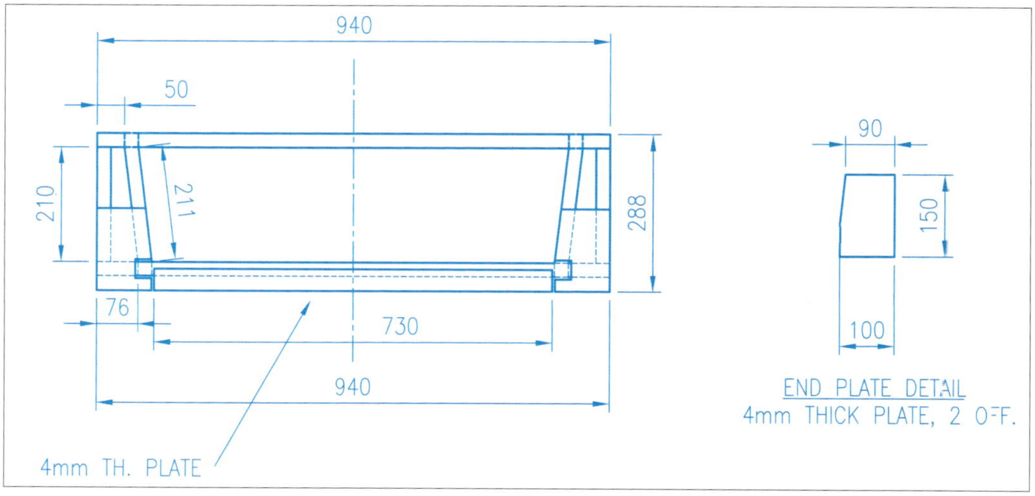

Drg 6.6g Chassis section F-F (see Drg 6.6). Dimensions in millimetres.

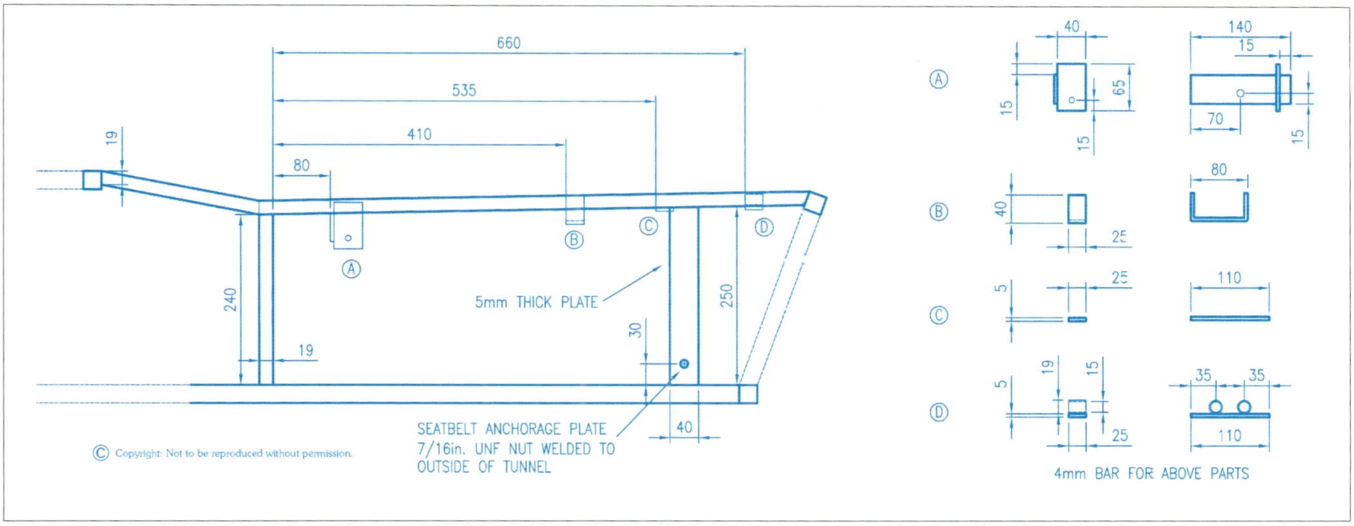

Drg 6.6h Chassis section H-H (see Drg 6.6). Dimensions in millimetres.

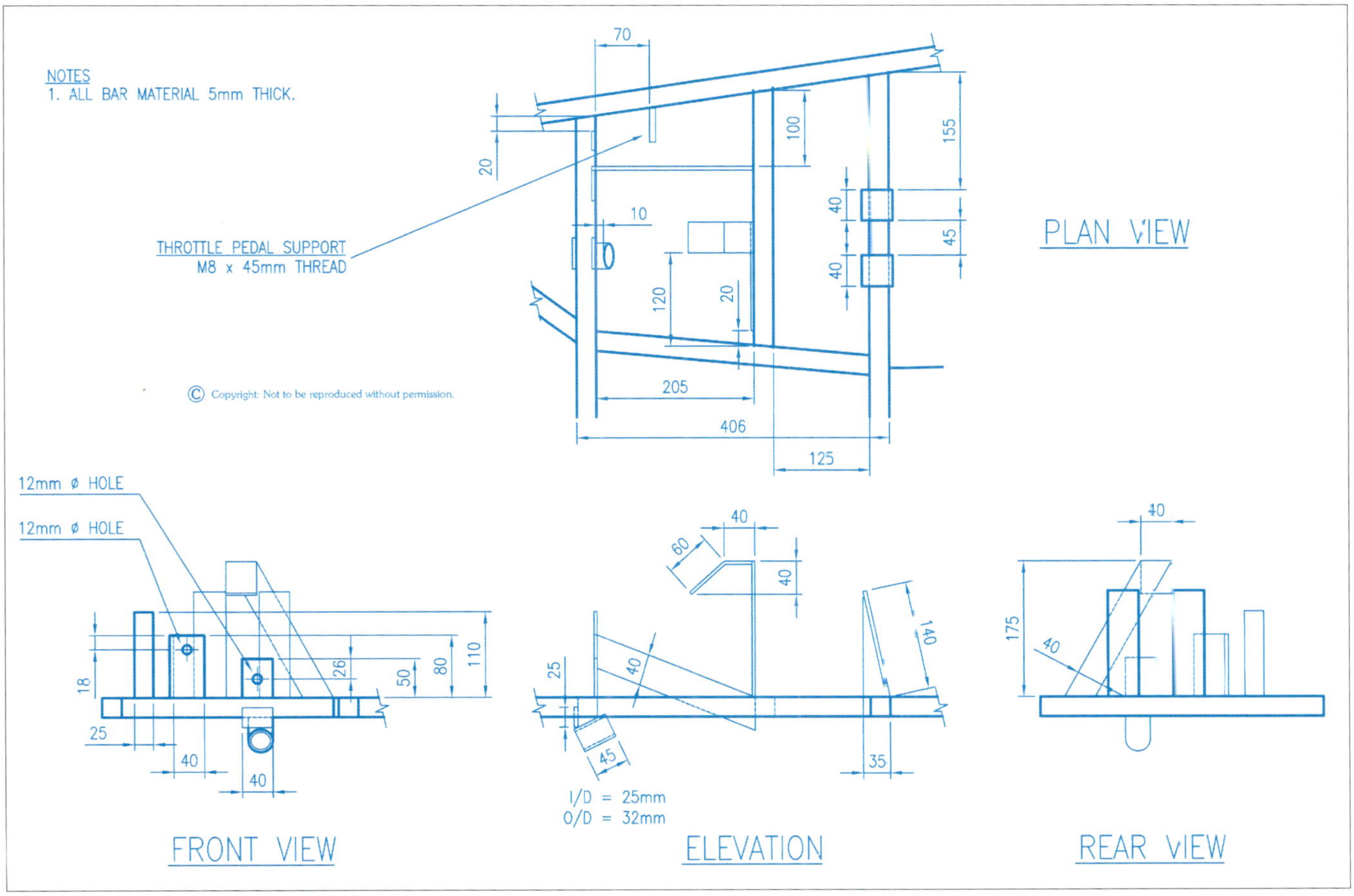

Drg 6.7 Tiger Avon chassis foot pedal and steering column support detail. Dimensions in millimetres.

Right & below: Side view and rear three-quarter view of Tiger Avon chassis.

Front three-quarter view of Tiger Avon chassis.

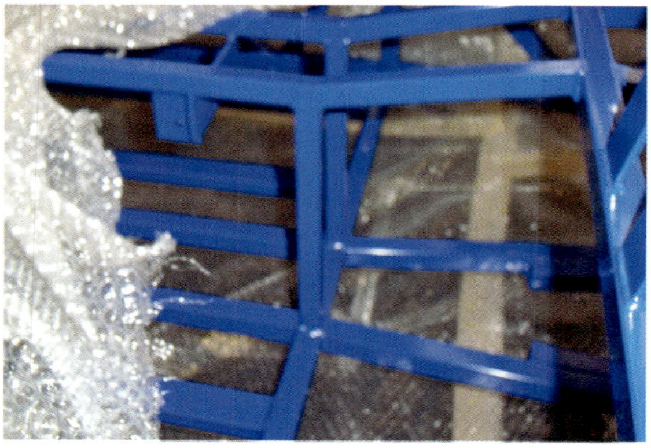

Later front tunnel tubes.

Side view of rear of Tiger Avon chassis showing suspension mountings.

Rear view of Tiger Avon chassis.

Side view of front of Tiger Avon chassis showing suspension mountings.

Top view of front of Tiger Avon chassis.

Top view of rear of Tiger Avon chassis.

Control pedal area of Tiger Avon chassis.

Top left & left: Overview of Tiger Avon chassis.

More views of control pedal area of Tiger Avon chassis.

The revised way of fitting Sierra pedals.

The new plate fitted and welded to the underside of the chassis to enable floor-mounted pedals to be fitted.

The small tab welded on the top rail to enable the nose to be bolted each side.

Need Tiger's help?
E-mail – Jim@tigerracing.com

Various suspension parts, the flat steel components have been laser cut.

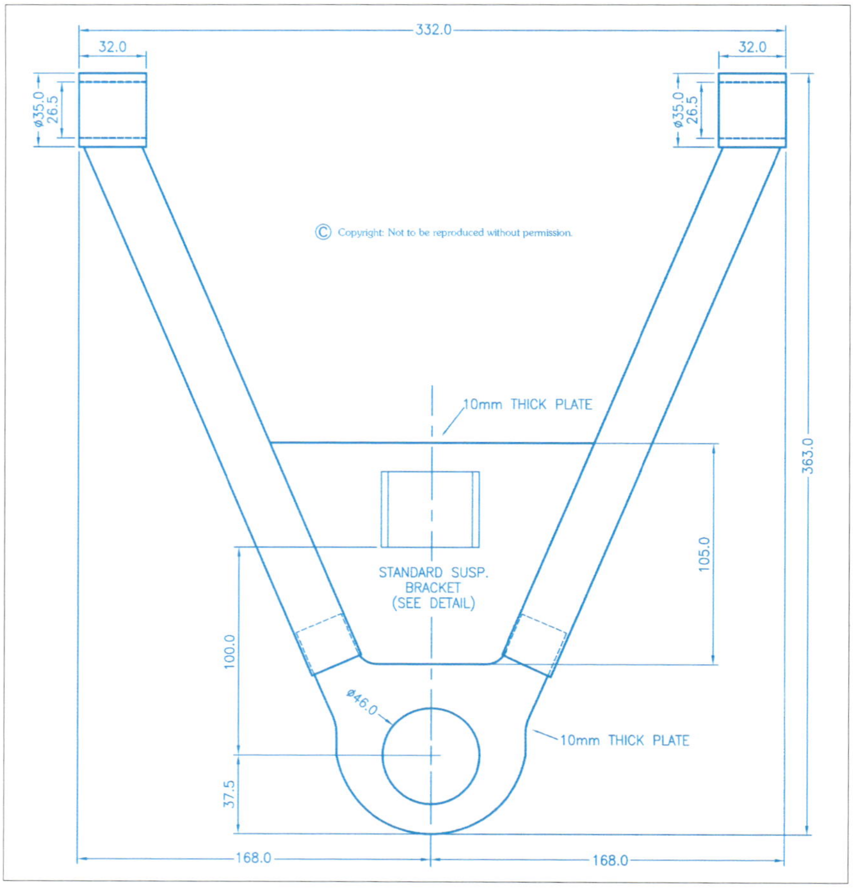

Drg 6.8a Tiger Avon front suspension bottom wishbone. Dimensions in millimetres.

A wishbone fabrication jig.

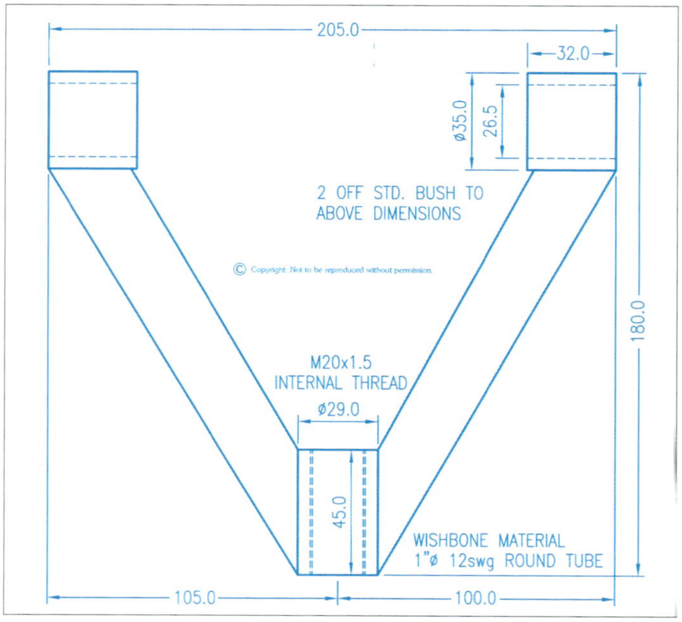

Drg 6.8b Tiger Avon front suspension top wishbone. Dimensions in millimetres.

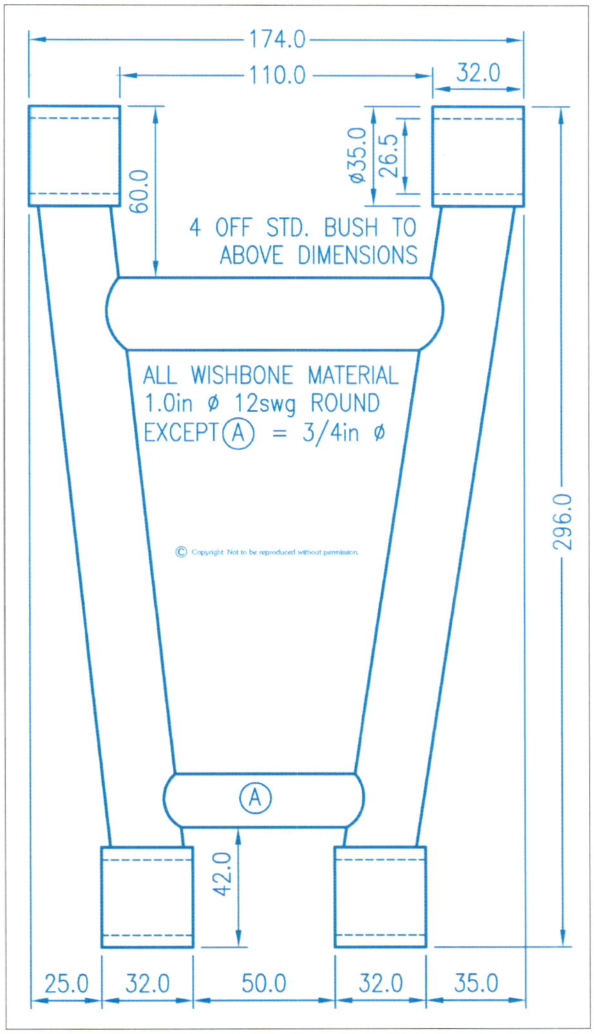

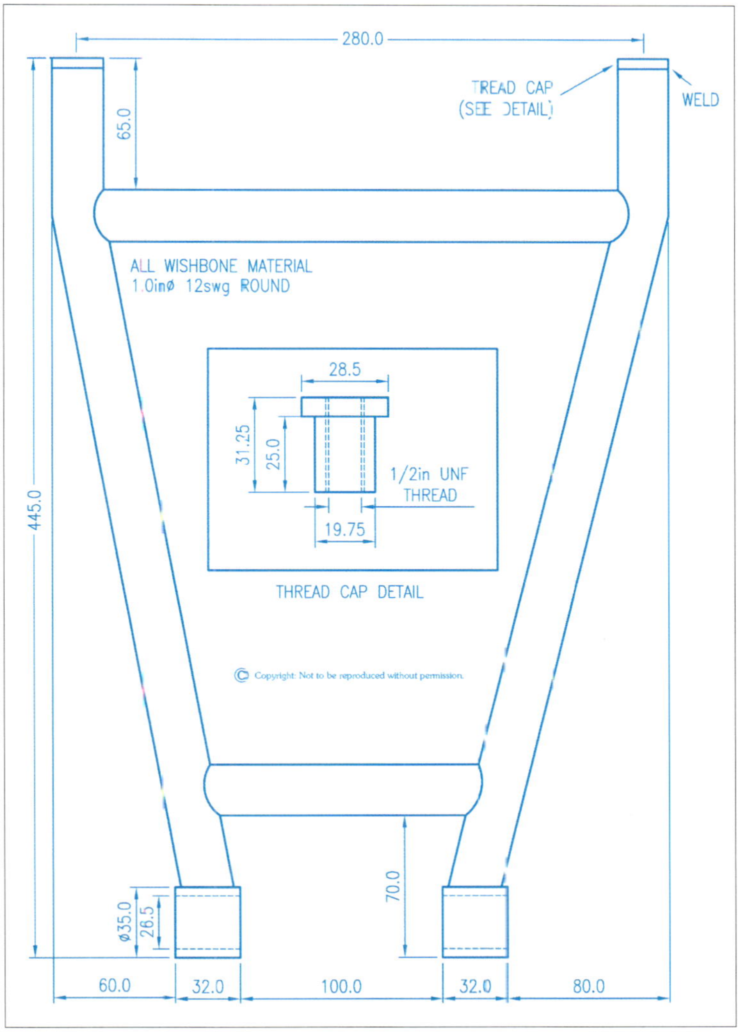

Drg 6.9a Tiger Avon rear suspension bottom wishbone. Dimensions in millimetres.

Above, right: Drg 6.9b Tiger Avon rear suspension top wishbone. Dimensions in millimetres.

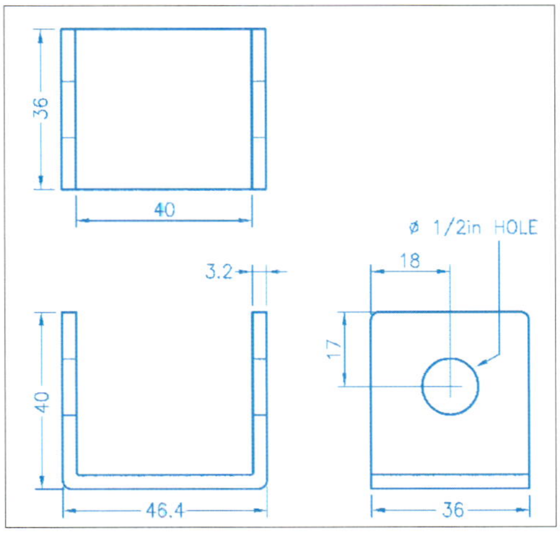

Drg 6.10 Tiger Avon standard suspension bracket. Dimensions in millimetres.

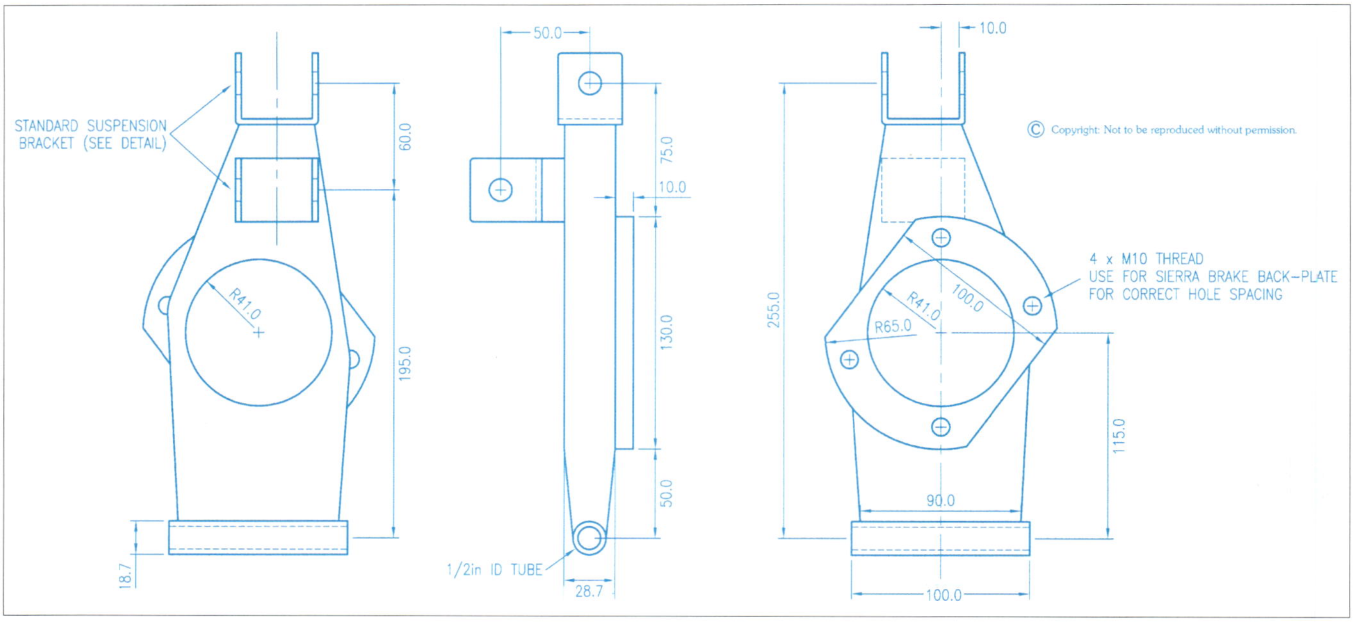

Drg 6.11 Tiger Avon rear suspension upright (hub carrier). Dimensions in millimetres.

The jigs used to fabricate left and right rear suspension uprights (hub carriers), with a completed upright in the centre. These are used for the smallest diameter 'push-in' Sierra drive shaft. If using a larger diameter drive shaft, the central tube section in the hub will need to be larger.

Chapter 7

IVA (Individual Vehicle Approval)

In the UK before 1998 you could have just taken your newly built sports car for a standard MoT test (the annual roadworthiness test in the UK) at your local garage: VOSA then introduced the SVA (Single Vehicle Approval) system, which has since been revised, upgraded and renamed. Since 2011, cars need to pass the new IVA (Individual Vehicle Approval) test before being allowed on the public highway. If you've built a Tiger Avon outside the UK, you'll need to check with your vehicle licensing authorities about how to have the car checked and confirmed as roadworthy and legally compliant.

When your car passes the UK IVA test, you'll be given a IAC (Individual Approval Certificate). The IVA test is over three hours longer than a standard MoT test, and the vehicle examiner will check not only the obvious things like steering and brakes but will also look at many aspects of the vehicle's design and build quality. The severity of the exhaust emissions part of the test will be based on the year of manufacture of the engine. As a guide if your engine is no newer that July 1995, it should require a less stringent emission level – check with VOSA before because you will have to declare the engine year on your application. Note that a catalytic convertor will be required for engines manufactured after August 1995.

At the time of writing this book, a great number of homebuilt Tigers had passed the previous SVA test and the current IVA test, so you shouldn't worry unduly about your car's ability to pass the test if you have built it properly.

If you have been building your car for some time – say over a few years – it's assumed that you initially read this section for the SVA test back when you started, so please note that there are some important amendments from the older SVA to the new IVA.

Should your car fail the test first time a re-test can usually be carried out within a week or two; this will give you time to sort out problems.

There are more than 15 IVA stations around the UK and, so long as you have an appointment card and insurance, you're allowed to drive to and from the chosen station without number (licence) plates.

For added peace of mind, Tiger offers a pre-IVA check and MoT, which can be booked a couple of weeks before the IVA test is due. An emission check can also be carried out, with a print-out of results, as well as setting suspension tracking. All these checks/settings can be carried out on the same day. Provided you're insured and have booked with Tiger under your chassis number, you're allowed to drive to the appointment without a registration number.

This chapter details the general requirements of the IVA test as they were at the time of writing. However, it's strongly recommended that you download the IVA Inspection Manual (details in appendix). Once you have a manual, it's a good idea to regularly check for updates to the requirements.

Readers building cars outside the UK will need to check with their local authorities regarding local regulations and roadworthiness tests. **Wherever you live, the IVA requirements make sense in terms of building a safe and reliable car.**

IVA TEST REQUIREMENTS (UK ONLY)

Anti-theft device

You'll need a steering lock – the standard Ford Sierra one will be fine for this part of the test. If you're not using the Sierra steering lock or one from another mass-production car, check the IVA manual.

Defrosting/demisting (defogging)

If fitting a full windscreen (windshield), you'll need a defrost/demist system. This is achieved by ducting warm air from the heater matrix up to the bottom of the windscreen, or by fitting a heated windscreen (contact Tiger for details). If no windscreen is fitted, no defrost is required.

Windscreen (windshield) wipers & washers

If a windscreen's fitted, the wipers must self park without obstructing the driver's view, sweep at 45 cycles per minute and have two speeds. The windscreen washer system must have a minimum of 1 litre capacity and must spray at a minimum pressure from the jets.

Seats & their fixings

For the Clubman-type car, the main requirement will be that the seats are securely fixed to the chassis and that headrests are fitted. For all other variations, check the IVA manual.

Seatbelts & their anchorages

The minimum requirement is three anchorages on the vehicle frame for seatbelts; two lower lap (for the lap belt) attached to the chassis, and one upper (for the shoulder harness). The upper seatbelt point is usually attached to the roll bar on the outer tube, and on certain chassis designs it can be attached to the top chassis rail – these chassis will have a much higher rear section behind the seating and can include two fixing points for 'four-point belts.' Since the SVA to IVA changes, 'static' three-point belts can no longer be used, but automatic three-point versions can. As previously mentioned, four-point harnesses can be used, but do check the required height of the anchorage points in the IVA manual; these are measured in relation to the height of the lower seat pad thickness.

Each of the anchorages must be (7⁄16in UNF) threaded, of the correct strength and positioned correctly (check the manual for positions).

Alternatively, the anchorage can comprise a steel tube passing through (protruding on both sides) and fully welded to the chassis rail. The tube must be capable of taking a bolt and locknut of at least equivalent strength to a 7⁄16in UNF bolt.

The seatbelt must also have the correct 'E' marks or their international equivalents – check these with IVA certification.

Interior fittings

In general, all interior fitting edges must have a radius of at least 2.5mm and the lower edge of dash a 19mm radius. Check all protrusion criteria in the current IVA manual as there are exemption areas.

Radio suppression

The HT ignition system must have radio suppression. The HT leads must also have type-approval marks.

Glazing

If a windscreen is fitted, your view of the road from the driving position must be unobstructed. Side screens can be removable but must be secured properly when in use. Windscreens must have an 'E' mark or equivalent.

Lighting

Check your IVA manual for full current requirements. Note that you'll be required to fit your car's lights between minimum and maximum heights and at required maximum distance from the outside of the body line of the car.

You car will require front and rear lights, indicator (turn signal) lights, repeater lights, foglight, reversing light and number (license) plate light.

You'll also need 'telltale' lamps for the dash panel (fascia) that must be marked with the correct symbol.

All lights need to meet a standard of brightness and angles of visibility requirements: check the IVA manual for current details.

Rear view mirrors

Rear view mirrors will be required to meet the 'field of view' requirements.

You'll need an interior mirror (with an 'E' mark) and an offside (right-hand side of car) exterior mirror outside the driving compartment. The radii on the mirror edges must be 2.5mm (0.098in) and, for the exterior mirror, there is a requirement that the mirror has a knock back facility so that it will rotate backwards when a force of 10kg is applied (this is not required if the mirror is inside the bodyline).

If the 'field of view' requirements cannot be met with an interior mirror and an offside mirror, fitting a nearside mirror too may help.

You should be able to adjust two mirrors from the driver's seat.

Check the IVA manual for all current requirements.

Tyres (tires)

Basically the tyres should have an 'e' or similar speed marking: if you're purchasing from a reputable tyre company or stockist the tyres will be legal, otherwise they would not be allowed to be sold.

Doors and catches

If you're designing a model with doors, check the IVA manual for current requirements, which will include two-stage door lock assembly and glass with the correct markings.

Exterior projections

To prevent personal injury, most edges and/or protrusions in and around the car will have to have a radius of 2.5mm (0.098in). There are too many instances to list here, so check the IVA manual for current requirements (note that the edges on the underside of your main bodywork [facing toward the ground] will also need a 2.5mm radius).

In general, all such edges should be rounded off to a radius of 2.5mm or covered with a U-shaped finisher or slit rubber hose: using tape and thin foam is **not** enough to pass the IVA test. Note that some sharp edges on the front hubs may also need to be filed/sanded to a 2.5mm radius (best done before they're painted and fitted).

Steering wheel & column

This section covers the steering column and steering wheel which must be designed to offer the driver a degree of protection from frontal impact. The steering wheel and its boss will need to be of an approved type. The steering shaft (from column to steering rack) will need offset universal joints. The IVA manual shows some approved types of shaft.

Basic design

This section of the IVA test covers the general design of the car and takes in many features like steering, wheels, chassis, mountings, suspension, fuel system, electrical and others.

The assessment includes a 10-15mph driving test of the car to ensure that there is a degree of self-centring in the steering. (It's worth noting that initially a lot of light clubman-type cars have poor self-centring until the tyres have bedded in).

Brakes

When the vehicle's braking is tested on rollers, the test will take into account the car's weight and the amount of pressure applied to the brake pedal. For full details of current braking requirements, please check the IVA manual.

Exhaust system

The exhaust system is checked for security of attachment and noise level. The noise level should not exceed 99dbA when the engine is run at approximately 66 per cent of its maximum speed.

Exhaust emissions

The exhaust emission requirement will be the statutory requirement in force in the year your car's engine was made.

Note that engines manufactured after August 1995 will require a catalytic converter in the exhaust system and, probably, fuel-injection (it's difficult to meet the later emissions standard with carburettor engines).

A full list of maximum permitted exhaust emission levels is printed in the IVA manual.

Speedometer

A speedometer is mandatory and it must have illumination. The speedometer's accuracy will be tested while the car is on the rollers. Note that electronic speedometers are available that you can calibrate at home before the test or, possibly, even adjust at the test centre.

Design weights

This section of the test has various calculations relating to design weights.

Manufacturer's plate

This relates to the chassis number given to the car. In the case of chassis purchased from Tiger, a 17 digit VIN (Vehicle Identification Number) will have been allocated by Tiger. These are found on a special alloy Tiger marked plate usually riveted to the inside of the bulkhead (dash). A matching VIN should be found under the bonnet (hood), stamped into a section of the chassis that can be read clearly by an IVA inspector.

Those who build their own chassis will have to visit their local VRO (Vehicle Registration Office) which will allocate a number.

VIN numbers must be displayed in accordance with IVA requirements.

Chapter 8
Assembly

ALUMINIUM PANELS

Note that 18-20swg is the recommended gauge for the aluminium sheet.

As a guide to making and fitting the aluminium panels see the accompanying illustrations. You'll also need to fabricate: 1) a battery tray which can be cut and shaped from a sheet 600mm (23.62in) x 420mm (16.53in); 2) two panels to close off under the rear wings which you can cut and shape from a sheet 520mm (20.47in) x 140mm (5.50in); 3) panels for closing off around the top central tunnel and cutting and fitting around the gearstick and handbrake lever which can be cut from a sheet 1250mm (49.21in) x 200mm (7.87in).

Caution! When cutting out your panels, don't cut away too much material initially, instead keep offering up the panel to the chassis and trim lightly until you achieve the best possible fit.

Some panels may need to be shaped to go around corners in the chassis. It's OK to butt edges and use

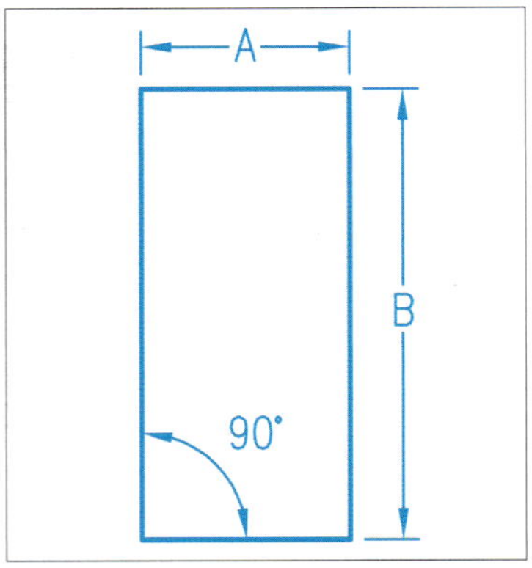

Drg 8.1 Tiger Avon floor panel (two required). A = 470mm (18.50in). B = 1300mm (51.18in).

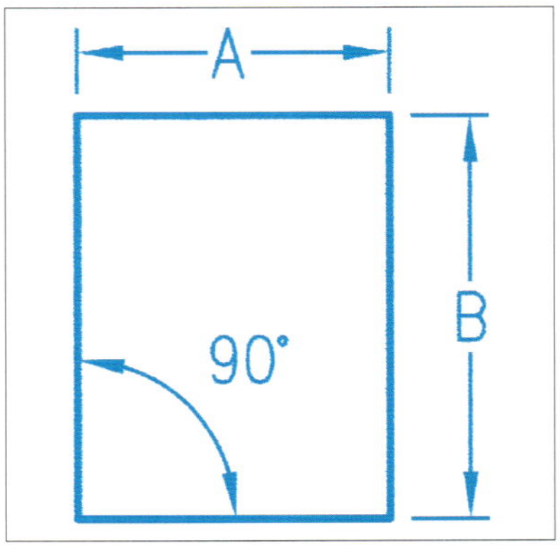

Drg 8.2 Tiger Avon front footwell panel (two required). A = 280mm (11.02). B = 335mm (13.18in).

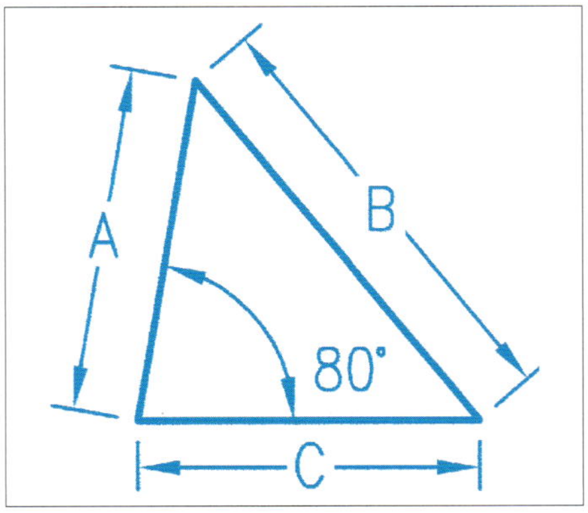

Drg 8.3 Tiger Avon inner rear wing (fender) panel (two required). A = 535mm (21.06in). B = 600mm (23.62in). C = 330mm (12.99in).

Using the top chassis rail as a former to bend aluminium sheet.

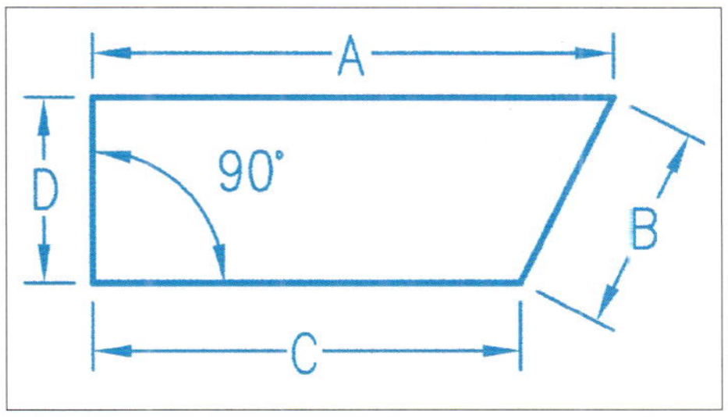

Drg 8.6 Tiger Avon rear inside tunnel panel (two required). A = 810mm (31.88in). B = 315mm (12.40in). C = 700mm (27.55in). D = 290mm (11.41in).

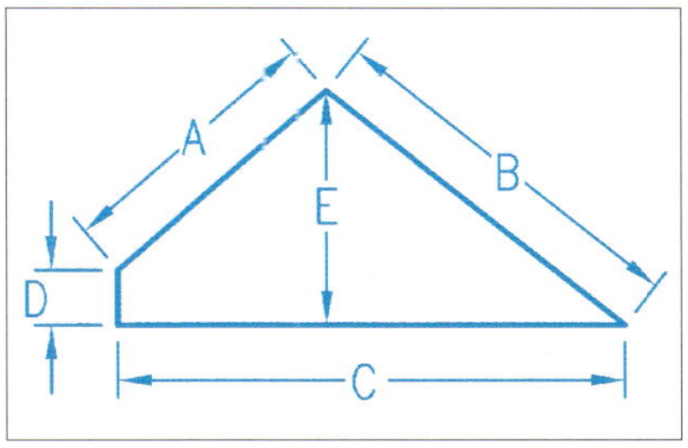

Drg 8.7 Tiger Avon inside, by seatbelt anchorage. panel (two required). A = 280mm (11.02in). B = 400mm (15.74in). C = 485mm (19.09in).

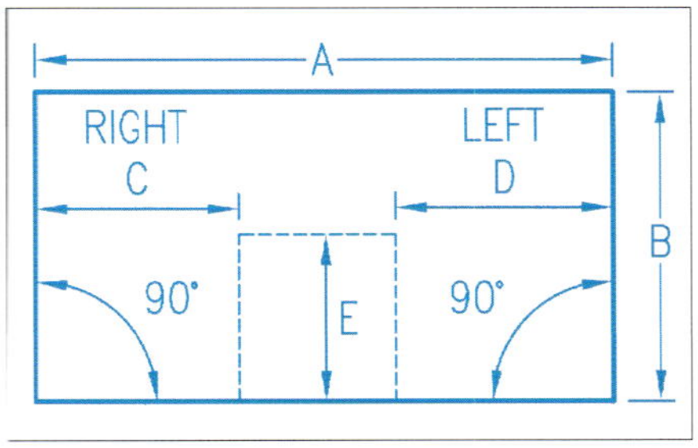

Drg 8.4 Tiger Avon seatback panel. A = 960mm (37.79in). B = 585mm (23.03in). E = (cut to fit).

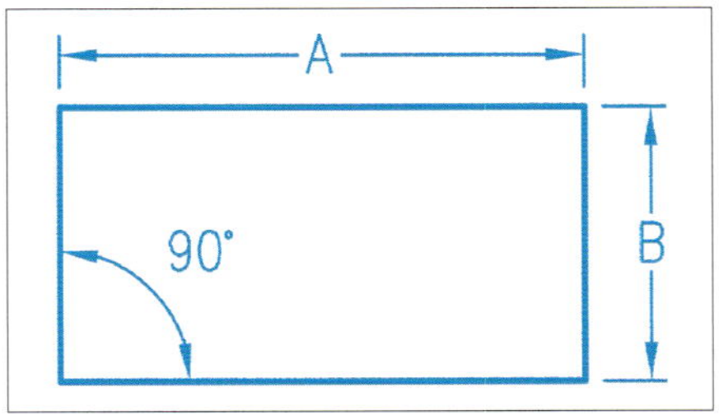

Drg 8.5 Tiger Avon front inside tunnel panel (two required). A = 585mm (23.03in). B = 335mm (13.18in).

adhesive in these corners (front footwell panels can be sealed this way where they butt the front tunnel). The top chassis rail can be used as a former to bend an aluminium panel through a 90 degree angle.

Warning! Ensure the edges of panels are smooth prior to final fitting.

Drill rivet holes through aluminium interior panel and chassis frame every 75mm (3in).

Drilling and riveting aluminium floor panels to chassis.

Seal corner joints with a bead of silicone sealant or with adhesive.

Panel fitting

To fit a finally shaped and trimmed panel, position it on the chassis and drill appropriately sized holes through the panel and chassis in each corner. Then temporarily pop (blind) rivet the panel to the chassis. Now drill holes through the panel and chassis approximately every 75mm (3in) around the panel's periphery.

Drill out the rivets from the corners of the panel and remove the panel. Using white spirit, or other cleaner, clean the panel and the chassis members to which the panel will be fitted. Apply a thin bead of silicone sealant to the chassis members.

Refit the panel and rivet it to the chassis in its correct position.

Clean off any silicone sealant that may have been squeezed out from under the panel.

FUEL TANK SENDER UNIT

Using a hole cutter, make a hole in the top of the fuel tank to suit the tank sender unit. Remember to allow for the length of the float arm when positioning the opening. It may be easier to cut the opening for the sender unit before the tank is fabricated.

Attach the float to the sender unit and place the whole unit into the opening situated in the top of the tank.

The float will probably be in contact with the bottom of the tank, but this is not advisable as it means the tank will be dry before the gauge reads empty. So, bend the float rod up a little so that the float is about 20mm (0.75in) above the bottom of the tank. You can hold the sender against the outside of the tank as a guide to float position at full droop.

With the fuel sender in place, using a punch or pen, mark where the holes need to be drilled which will take the unit's securing screws.

Drill holes of a suitable size for self-tapping screws. **Caution!** Be careful not to leave any metal filings inside the tank.

Fit the sender and tighten the self-tapping screws to secure it in place. **Warning!** Don't forget the gasket.

FUEL TANK

The tank can be secured by welding two 40mm (1.6in) wide pieces of steel 5mm (0.20in) thick across the bottom of the new tank (**Warning!** On no account weld a tank that has had fuel inside).

Sender unit of Tiger Avon fuel tank.

Fuel tank supported by 40mm x 5mm (1.57 x 0.19in) straps welded to its underside and bolted to the chassis.

Large diameter fuel filler rubber pipe and the small diameter breather pipe (which goes up to the side of the filler neck).

Fuel tank filler neck stub.

Next, drill the supports and the rear lower 1in chassis tubes so that the straps can be bolted to the chassis. Alternatively, make two metal straps to encircle the tank (a thin strip of rubber between strap and tank is advisable) and fix them to the chassis.

FUEL LINE

If it has been coiled, gently straighten out the 0.25in (6.3mm) rigid fuel line piping. Note that if fuel-injection is used, you'll need two fuel pipes (one feed and one return) of 8mm size. **Warning!** Fuel-injection systems have very high pressures in the fuel lines, so make sure you use high pressure compression joints.

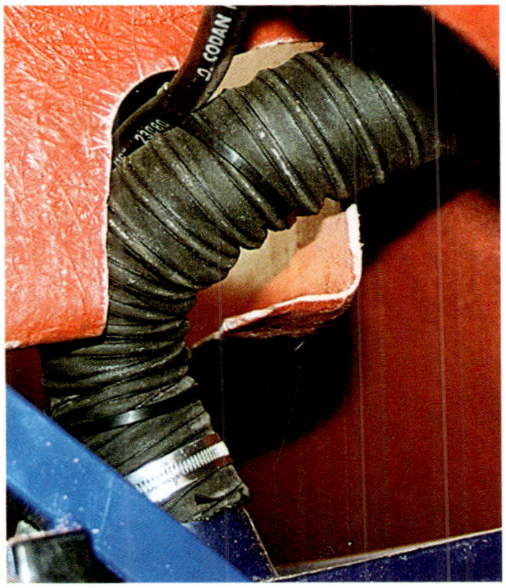

View of fuel filler & breather pipes from under rear wing (fender).

Place the fuel line piping into the transmission tunnel and bend it into shape so it runs close to the chassis members to which it will be fixed. Ensure the fuel line extends well past the rear of the transmission tunnel and will reach the loose end of the flexible pipe (or pipes) running between the fuel tank and line. It's best to use pipe benders to shape the fuel line: it can be bent by hand, but be very careful not to collapse a section of the line.

Fuel filler cap. The flush-fitting 'Aero' type can also be used.

Now the fuel line pipe needs

to be fixed to the chassis members. This is done with the use of plastic P-clips and pop (blind) rivets (see the accompanying illustration of brake line fixing which uses the same method).

Warning! Ensure that no part of the fuel line is touching any sharp edges or moving parts.

BRAKE LINES & BRAKE REGULATOR

Components

You'll need the following rigid brake piping with unions –

Master cylinder to rear compensator: 1840mm (72.44in) long, male-male.

Regulator to T-piece: 250mm (9.84in) long, male-male.

Right-hand side rear from T-piece to flexible hose: 260mm (10.23in) long, male-female.

Left-hand side rear from T-piece to flexible hose: 850mm (33.46in) long, male-female.

Right-hand side front from master cylinder to flexible hose: 1070mm (42.12in) long, male-female.

Left-hand side front from master cylinder to flexible hose: 1960mm (77.16in) long, male-female.

You'll also need –

1 x T-piece, ex Sierra, (all female)

1 x brake regulator (donor Sierra unit is fine)

Regulator

A brake regulator (compensator) will be required to reduce braking force to the rear brakes (**Warning!** Rear brakes should never be allowed to lock-up before the front brakes). This device is fitted between the master cylinder and the rear brakes, clear of any moving parts. Fit the regulator in the same sort of angle and orientation as

Brake regulator (compensator) from a Ford Sierra.

Rigid brake line running through central tunnel.

Flexible brake hose between body and front brake caliper.

Rigid brake piping fixed to chassis with P-clips.

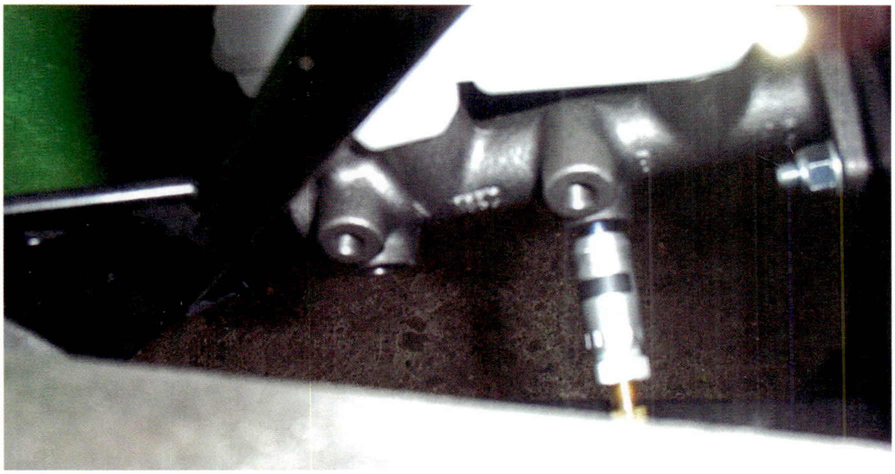

Master cylinder with a brake regulator valve fitted on the outlet to the rear brakes. There is also a brakelight switch fitted, which is usually on the other outlet next to the regulator. The front two outlets are for left and right front brake pipes.

it was fitted in the Sierra. Rear brake efficiency can be tested at your local MoT station. Very modern cars have a small restrictor/regulator. This can be fitted directly into the rear exit on the master cylinder, with the rear brake pipe fitted into restrictor/regulator and then returned to the rear brakes.

Note that if you're building a live axle car, it is quite possible that the wheel (slave) cylinders fitted to the rear brakes will be designed to restrict the rear braking force, so a brake regulator may not be required.

Rigid brake lines are secured to the chassis members by the same means as the fuel lines (P-clips). Four flexible brake pipes will be required, unless you're using a live rear axle, in which case only three will be needed.

One pipe will run through the chassis central tunnel (see accompanying photo) from the master cylinder into the brake regulator and then into a T-piece. From the rear T-piece, two short pieces of rigid pipe will run out to each side to meet the flexible hoses from the individual rear brakes. At the front, from the master cylinder two brake pipes will go around the chassis (see accompanying illustrations) to the flexible hoses from the front callipers.

The male connector of each front flexible brake hose will pass through the bodywork and be secured on the inside (engine side) by a nut. When the flexible hose is securely fixed to the body, the rigid brake pipe can be attached to it.

The male connectors at the inboard end of the rear brake flexible hoses will be held in brackets welded to the chassis.

ROLL BAR

Place the roll bar onto the top of the rear chassis member and use the base plate holes to mark and drill the four (10mm) holes through the chassis. Secure the roll bar with 8.8 ton 10mm bolts and locknuts.

Roll bar mounting to chassis. Note seatbelt anchorage.

LIVE REAR AXLE OPTION

The chassis drawings in this book are for a car with independent rear suspension. However, we'd like you to have as many options as possible so, maybe, as well as a self-designed GRP body you'll want to use a live rear axle? Probably the easiest way of doing this is with a five link system: this comprises four trailing arms and a Panhard rod.

You'll need to remove the old locating brackets on your chosen axle, and make and weld on new ones to locate the five link system.

The trailing arms are connected at one end to the chassis and at the other to links above and below the axle. The trailing arms should be parallel with each other and, ideally, parallel with the ground when the vehicle is at normal loaded ride height.

The Panhard rod should be as long as possible, with one end as close to the centre of the axle as possible. Again, ideally, the Panhard rod should be parallel with the ground when the vehicle is at normal loaded ride height.

The trailing arms and Panhard rod will require bushes to be fitted, and you can press in the new bushes using a vice (vise) or press. Nylon bushes are now fitted to many track/fast road cars, and these are available at little additional cost.

Fitting of trailing arms

It's recommended that you put the axle into place in the chassis before fitting the trailing arms and Panhard rod.

Place the trailing arms into the brackets on the chassis and the axle.

Grease all bolts before fitting.

Trailing arms and brackets on a live axle Tiger Super Six.

Live axle with new trailing arm brackets welded in place.

Adjustable length trailing arms with bushes and Rose joints.

Push bolts through chassis brackets and trailing arms, making sure that the bolt head faces the inside of the car.

Place one end of the Panhard rod into the bracket on the chassis. Place the other end into the bracket on the rear axle.

Warning! Use locknuts on all bolts.

FITTING SUSPENSION BUSHES

The method for fitting bushes is the same for wishbones, trailing arms and Panhard rods. You can use a vice (vise) or a press.

Coat the outer surface of the bush and inner surface of the housing with washing-up liquid (check for any burrs on the inside of the housing and remove). Line up the correct end of the bush (there's usually a taper on the steel or rubber bush) with the arm and place both into the vice.

Tighten the vice jaws, forcing the bush into the arm (applying more washing-up liquid if required). When the bush has entered the housing so far it will bottom out against the vice: to overcome this problem a sleeve (or a socket) with the same internal diameter as the arm is used. Release the bush and arm from the vice and place the sleeve or socket between the arm and the vice. Tighten the vice jaws until the bush is completely inserted into the arm with the shoulders showing equally on each side of the housing.

The bushes can of course be fitted with a press if you have access to one, the method is the same.

FRONT BALL JOINT (LOWER)

The lower ball joint is placed on top of the wishbone and the three (8mm) holes marked and drilled. Bolt the ball joint to the wishbone with 12.9-ton (min.) cap head bolts with locknuts.

Tiger Avon lower ball joint.

Ford Cortina-type suspension upright and hub assembly on a Tiger Avon. Note split pin in upper ball joint.

FRONT BALL JOINT (UPPER)

Take the top ball joint and screw the locknut onto it. Then screw the ball joint into the top wishbone (see illustrations).

FRONT WISHBONES

The wishbones are fitted to the chassis using 8.8 ton 0.5 x 2.5in bolts.

Warning! Use locknuts.

FRONT SUSPENSION UPRIGHTS (FORD CORTINA-TYPE)

The standard front supension upright/stub axle and wheel hub/disc assembly for the Avon are taken from the Ford Cortina Mk4/5. Before fitting, check the condition of the bearings and all threaded holes.

The hub upright locates on the

bottom and top ball joints of the wishbones.

The ball joint pins are tapered and slight pressure on the joints should stop them rotating as you tighten the securing nuts. **Warning!** Use locknuts to secure. **Warning!** Some top ball joints have the correct taper but the nylon in the locknut is only just engaging when the nut tightens. If you find this problem, after tightening the nut, drill a very small hole (2.5mm/0.010in) through both nut and pin and insert a split pin for safety.

Top ball joint and locknut.

FRONT SUSPENSION UPRIGHTS (FORD SIERRA-TYPE)

The most straightforward fitting for the Avon is the Ford Cortina upright (complete with hub and disc) used with the standard fabricated wishbones. However, you can use Sierra uprights/hubs as shown in the accompanying illustration if you're prepared to make a lot of chassis and suspension modifications. The arrangement uses a top rocker with shock absorbers mounted inside the chassis (like many single seater racing cars), and uses the standard Ford track control arm. Part of the original MacPherson strut suspension leg is used with a special taper bored component welded into the top. A ball joint screwed into the rocker attaches to the top of the modified upright.

Modified Sierra suspension upright/hub on a Tiger Cat (with a rocker arm-type suspension system).

Front suspension unit installed.

This Escort steering rack has extension pieces fitted to compensate for increased track. Warning! It's dangerous to use the standard unmodified tie rods as there will only be a few threads engaging the trackrod ends.

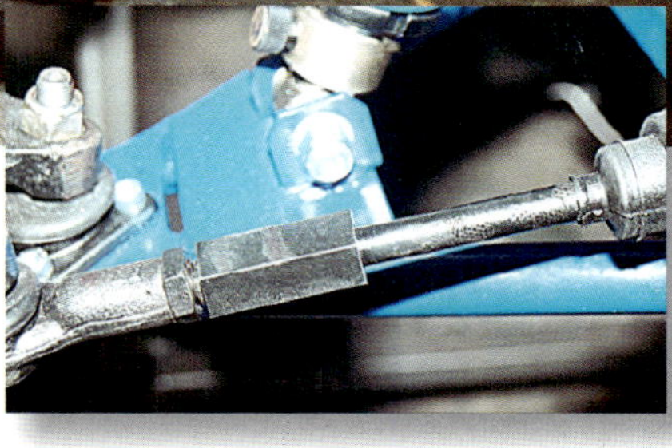

Close-up of correctly modified tie rod on an Escort rack.

FRONT AND REAR SPRING/SHOCK ABSORBER UNITS

The co-axial-type spring/shock absorber units (dampers) are secured to chassis and lower wishbone by 8.8 ton 0.5 x 2.5in bolts. **Warning!** Use locknuts.

Unmodified Sierra steering shaft.

STEERING RACK

Warning! The Ford Escort Mk2 steering rack will need a modification to extend the tie rods each side by 10-15mm (0.4-0.6in) to enable the trackrod ends to engage with enough tie rod threads for safety. This modification must be carried out by a professional engineer or by Tiger. Tiger can now supply new

Sierra steering shaft modified for use in a Tiger Avon.

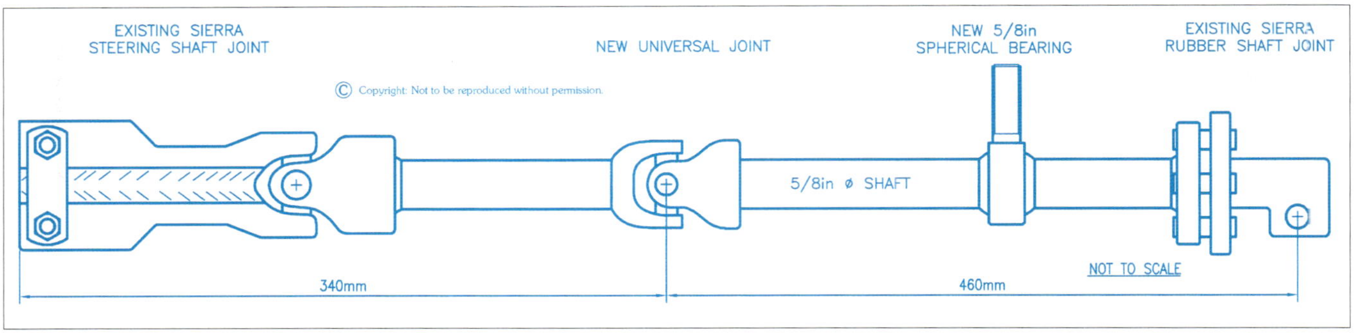

Drg 8.8 Modification to the Sierra steering shaft for Tiger Avon. Warning! This modification must be carried out by a qualified engineer.

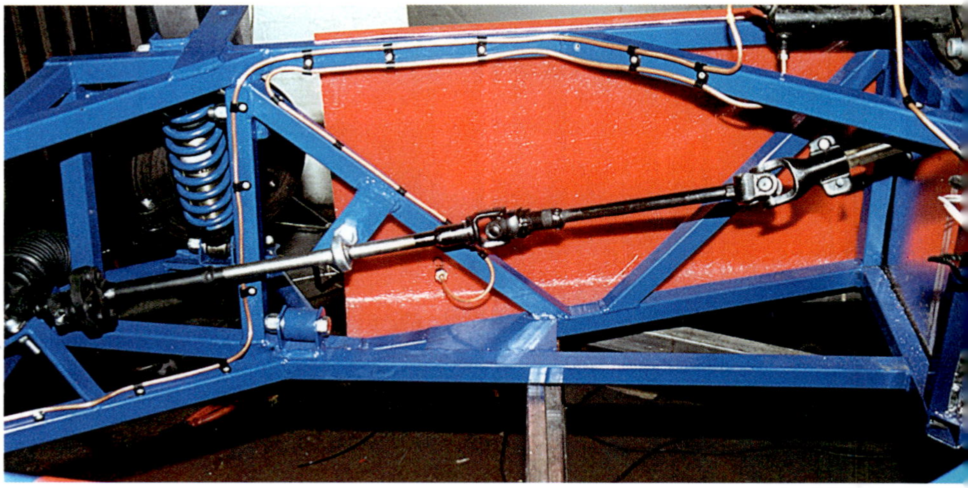

The steering column/shaft installed in a Tiger Avon chassis. Note how the Rose joint supports the steering shaft.

steering racks with tie rods of the correct length.

The steering rack is bolted to the chassis using two U-shaped steel clamps with rubber bushes under them. 8mm bolts are used (**Warning!** Use locknuts).

STEERING SHAFT

The modified Sierra steering shaft (see accompanying illustration) will bolt to the steering rack using a 12.9 ton 8mm cap head bolt and onto the bottom of the steering column with another bolt of the same specification. **Warning!** Use locknuts as necessary.

Warning! Steering shaft modifications must only be made by a qualified engineer; alternatively, you can buy a complete new shaft from Tiger.

The Rose joint on the steering shaft will attach to the bracket on the driver's side of the chassis. **Warning!** Use a locknut on the outside of the Rose joint securing bracket.

STEERING WHEEL AND BOSS

A type approved steering wheel and boss is required to pass the IVA test.

REAR SUSPENSION UPRIGHTS (HUB CARRIERS)

Each rear upright is secured to the top and bottom wishbones by long 0.5in diameter 8.8 ton bolts. The upper bolt needs to be 140mm (5.5in) long, the lower 204mm (8in). **Warning!** Use locknuts.

REAR WISHBONES

The rear lower wishbones pivot inboard on 0.5in Rose joints secured to the chassis brackets by 0.5in 8.8 ton bolts (66mm/2.5in long). Spacers fabricated from round steel tube (16swg walls) and cut to the correct length will need to be used to hold the Rose joints in correct position within the chassis brackets to align the wishbone as shown in accompanying drawing. Upper wishbones are secured to the chassis brackets by 0.5in 8.8 ton bolts of 64mm/2.5in length. **Warning!** Secure all bolts with locknuts.

DIFFERENTIAL UNIT

Position the differential unit between the four mounting brackets in the centre of the rear of the chassis and secure using long 200mm/7.9in long 12mm 8.8 ton bolts. **Warning!** Use locknuts.

CONTROL PEDALS

Ford Sierra pedals are used as standard for the Tiger Avon. If you're using the

Brake 'T'-piece fitted on alloy behind seats.

Avon rear hub fitted with nylon suspension bushes.

Tube with 0.5in inside diameter is cut and used for spacers between the bracket on the chassis and the rose joint.

Above: Rear suspension wishbones and hub carrier loosely fitted. Note visible spacer on inboard lower pivot and also the spacer between top outer hub bracket (between outer wishbone bushes).

Above right: Tiger Avon rear suspension fabricated lower wishbone.

Complete rear suspension installation on a Tiger Avon.

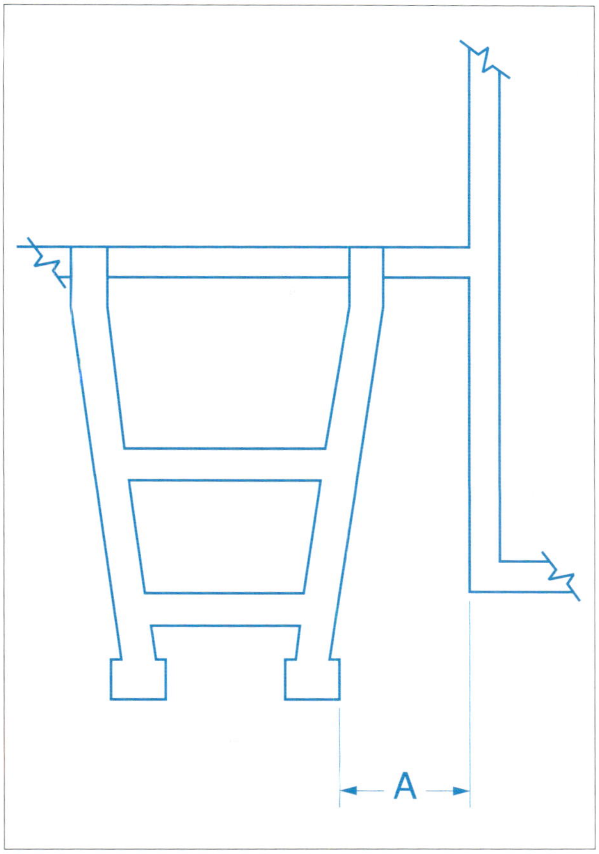

Drg 8.9 – Aprox position of rear wishbone.
A = 80mm (3.14in)

Sierra pedal box bolted into position in Tiger Avon chassis.

Ford Sierra differential unit secured to Tiger Avon chassis by long 12mm bolts.

Right: Modified Sierra brake pedal.

Far right: A Willwood brand adjustable pedal assembly fitted to a racing Tiger B6. You can also use aftermarket pedals in the Tiger Avon.

Above: The floor-mounted pedal system. The plate across the chassis uprights holds the master cylinder and also becomes the 'stop' for the outer clutch cable. It is possible to fit another master cylinder in this plate for a hydraulic clutch.

Above right: The 6mm thick plate bolted to the chassis uprights to house the master cylinder.

Pedal cover (note the access panel).

Above left: Pedal box cover (to cover Sierra pedals).

The 3.2mm (⅛in) steel plate welded into the driver's floor; brackets for the pedals are bolted to it.

Another view of the pedals. Note the 90-degree small steel bracket bolted to the floor in front of the brake pedal: this will prevent the pedal falling towards the driver.

standard chassis, the pedals will need to be modified to give more legroom and inter-pedal spacing.

Normally it's only necessary to modify the brake pedal by removing V-shaped sections from around the centre of the pedal with a hacksaw. The pedal is then bent, closing the 'V' and welded.

As an alternative to modified Sierra pedals you can use a floor-mounted pedal system. The Avon chassis must have a steel plate with a minimum thickness of 3.2mm (⅛in) welded to the front floor area to support the pedals. This setup usually provides more room for the taller driver.

BRAKE MASTER CYLINDER

The standard early Ford Sierra master cylinder (usually pre-1987), can be used in conjunction with standard Sierra pedals. A new master cylinder pushrod will need to be used as the Sierra servo is not used in the Avon (see drawing on page 100 of new master cylinder pushrod). The later Sierra (after 1987) can be used but allowance will have to be made when welding the brackets on the chassis as the hole centres are closer together. The pushrod is designed to fit between the Sierra master cylinder and the Sierra pedal assembly. Note that to gain more legroom, you can shorten the new pushrod (master cylinder end: 'A' in Drg 8.10). A 10mm locknut is screwed on to the new rod inside the pedal, the smaller diameter end of the rod going through the existing holes in the pedal.

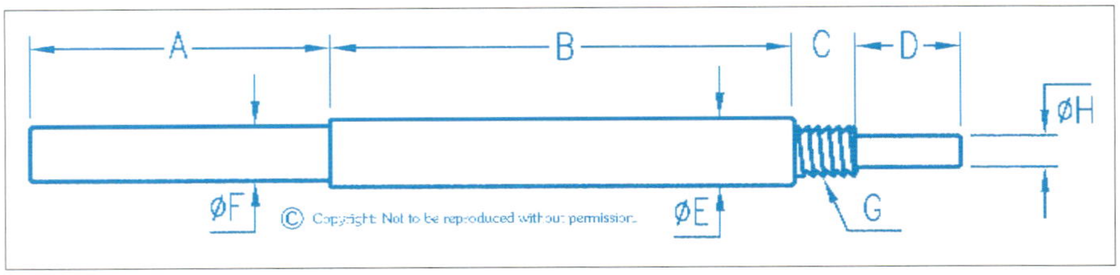

Drg 8.10 – Tiger Avon brake master cylinder pushrod dimensions. A = 60mm (2.36in). B = 95mm (3.74in). C = 10mm (0.39in). D = 20mm (0.78in). E = 12mm (0.47in) diameter. F = 10mm (0.39in) diameter. G = 10mm thread. H = 6mm (0.23in) diameter.

HANDBRAKE (PARKING BRAKE) LEVER

The standard Ford Sierra handbrake lever is used and fits centrally on the top of the transmission tunnel. Two 8.8 ton 8mm bolts are used (**Warning!** With locknuts) to secure the lever.

The two outer handbrake cables will push into the two tubular stops welded to the chassis just behind the handbrake lever. The standard Sierra inner cable is cut to separate it into two, the two inner cables fit into the made up balance bar (see illustration) and cable locks are used to secure them (see illustrations).

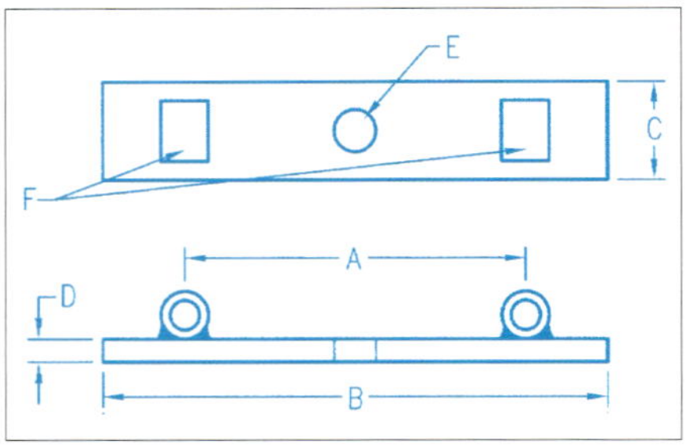

Drg 8.11 – Tiger Avon handbrake balance bar dimensions. A = 50mm (1.96in) (5mm/0.19in diameter holes in the two welded lugs). B = 75mm (2.95in). C = 25mm (0.98in). D = 5mm (1.96in). E = 8mm (0.31in). F = Steel tube.

Brake master cylinder in position. Note rigid brake lines fixed to chassis with P-clips.

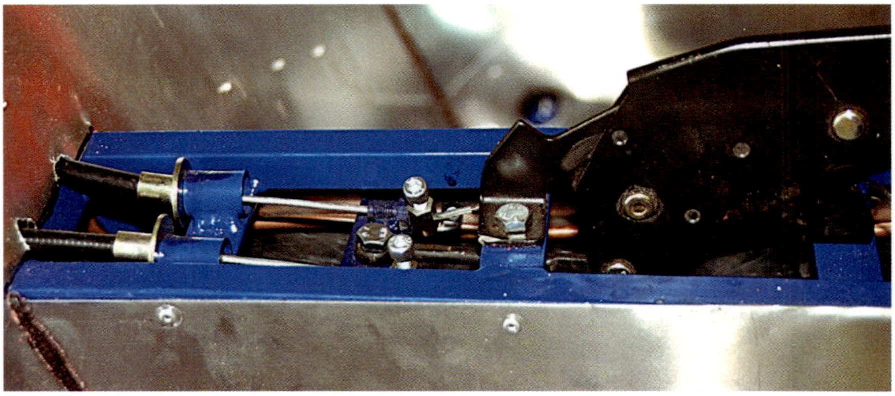

Handbrake (parking brake) lever mounted on Tiger Avon chassis and ...

... here a close-up of the outer cable stops, balance bar and lever pullrod.

Underside of front body fixed to Tiger Avon chassis by rivets.

BODYWORK

The standard Avon bodywork clips over the round section tube on the chassis near the seat area. The sides of the bodywork clip under the lower chassis rail and onto the top rail. Some of the GRP around the top rail, near where the roll bar is going to be fitted, needs to be removed (see illustration), as does some GRP over the round section near were you get in and out of the car.

The GRP is fixed to the chassis by drilling and pop (blind) riveting with 3.2mm (⅛in) rivets (**Warning!** Don't rivet where you get in and out of the car).

Underside of rear body fixed to Tiger Avon chassis by rivets.

Tiger Avon rear wing (fender).

Some of the body's GRP needs to be removed where the roll bar is going to be fitted to the chassis top rail.

A small section of GRP in the area of the side panel/rear wing (fender) joint needs to be removed as shown here.

Bonnet latch carbon fibre covers (on a Tiger Super Six).

Use the accompanying drawing as a guide to dashpanel position. The rear of the body (lower bottom edge) on the back panel is positioned level with the top of the lowest rearmost horizontal chassis tube: you can weld or rivet a piece of flat steel bar to this chassis member upon which the body can sit and be riveted to.

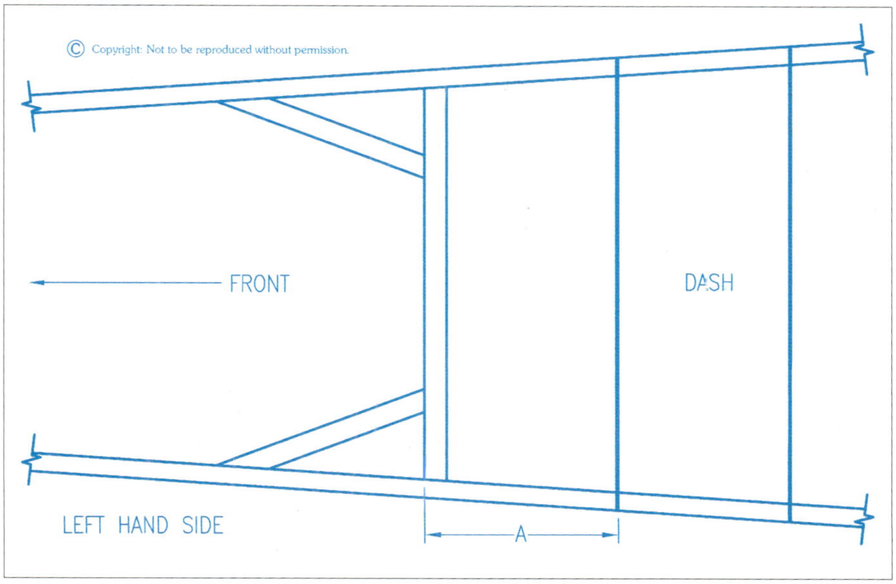

Drg 8.12 – Dashpanel (fascia) position relative to Tiger Avon chassis. A = 240mm (9.448in).

BONNET (HOOD) & NOSE

The bonnet rests on the dashpanel and on the nose. A seal can be put on the lips of both panels to rest the bonnet on. A bolt is then fitted through the tabs to hold the front of the nose (see page 77, bottom left). Four latches are used to hold the bonnet in place and these must not have any sharp edges, otherwise an IVA failure will result. Carbon fibre covers are available for these latches and will allow them to pass the IVA test.

TWIN SIDEDRAUGHT CARBURETTORS/ ELECTRIC FUEL PUMP

It is recommended that you install an electric fuel pump if you're going to use twin sidedraught carburettors. For neatness, the opening in the cylinder block where the original mechanical pump was fitted should have a blanking plate fitted over it. This plate can be made from a piece of flat metal and a fuel pump gasket used to seal the joint.

Simple blanking plate over mechanical fuel pump mounting. Note that a gasket must be used.

ENGINE AND GEARBOX (TRANSMISSION) INSTALLATION

Assembling the clutch

Caution! It's advisable to use a new clutch (friction disc and cover/pressure plate) unless the donor vehicle items are virtually as new. The flywheel face also needs to be in good condition. You must ensure that no oil or grease gets onto the friction plate or flywheel (clean the flywheel face with thinners).

Place the friction disk against the flywheel, ensuring the correct side (usually marked) faces the flywheel.

Place the clutch cover over the friction plate and onto the dowels protruding from the flywheel face.

Insert the bolts (with their spring washers) and do them up finger tight so that the friction plate may still be moved.

High capacity electric fuel pump for twin sidedraught carburettors fitted to a Tiger Super 6.

Clutch on a Ford 'Pinto' SOHC engine: this particular flywheel has had quite a lot of material taken off to lighten it.

Gearbox (transmission) mounting (Sierra with pan removed) viewed from above.

Crankshaft spigot bearing supports gearbox input shaft.

Using a clutch alignment tool, align the friction disc centre with the spigot bearing in the flywheel and then tighten the clutch cover securing bolts in rotation and one turn at a time. It's possible to fit the clutch without an alignment tool by leaving the clutch cover securing bolts finger tight then, with an assistant, push the gearbox onto the engine and up onto its dowels. Now, in one steady movement, slide the gearbox off the engine making sure it comes away squarely. It should now be safe to tighten the clutch cover bolts in rotation one turn at a time and then refit the engine.

Fitting gearbox (transmission) to engine

Lightly grease the input shaft spline of the gearbox.

Line up the engine and gearbox and then push the gearbox bellhousing onto the locating dowels in the engine block.

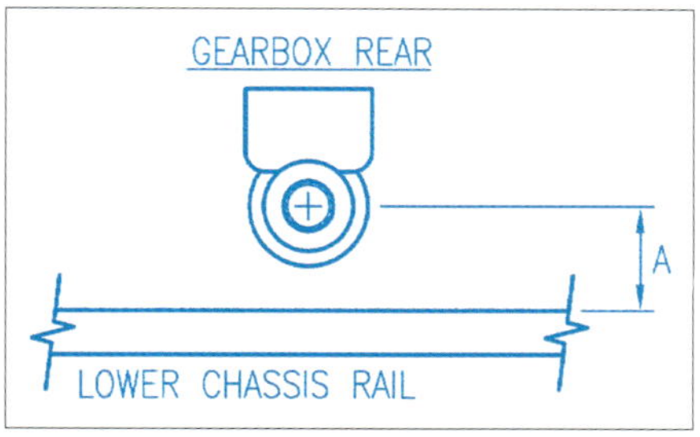

Drg 8.13 – Correct position of gearbox (transmission) relative to chassis. A = 120mm (4.724in).

Insert the M10 x 35 bolts (except starter bolts and one top bell housing bolt for the earth [ground] strap), and tighten.

Bolt the rear gearbox mounting to the chassis (see photo).

Note regarding fwd engines

Caution! If you're fitting an engine from a front-wheel drive car (*eg:* Ford Zetec 16v) remember you **must** fit a spigot bearing (from a manual transmission Sierra) in the rear of the crankshaft to support the gearbox input (first motion) shaft. Remember, too, to check that the dowels in the engine block (which locate the gearbox bellhousing precisely) are of the correct size. Also check the spline size on the gearbox input shaft in relation to the clutch friction plate spline size.

Fitting engine & gearbox (transmission)

The following text relates to the installation of the Tiger Avon's standard Ford SOHC 'Pinto' engine, but the procedure will be similar for other similar sized car engines.

Using an engine crane the engine is lowered into the car (with the gearbox attached) at around a 45 degree angle. When the gearbox is well down into the engine bay, lift its rear end onto the two small box sections inside the central

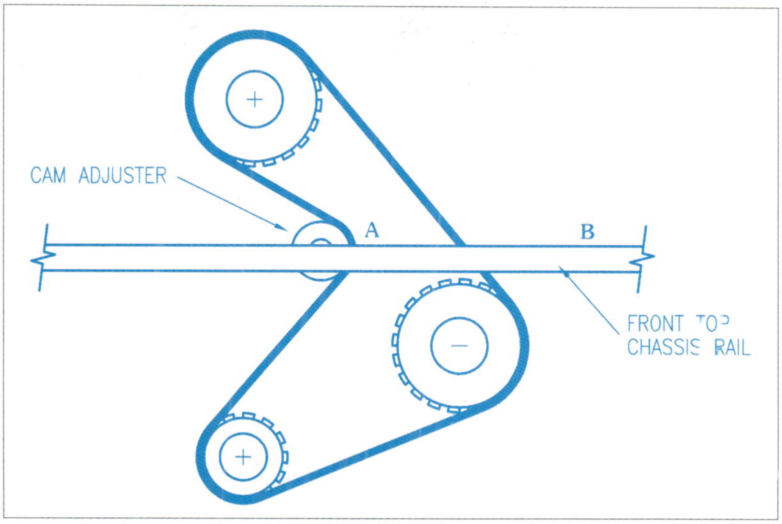

Drg 8.14 – Correct position of Ford 'Pinto' engine relative to chassis. A = cambelt adjuster. B = chassis rail top. Position = top of (B) through centre of (A).

Tiger Avon gearbox mounting arrangement.

tunnel. Fit the steel engine mounts onto the engine and lower onto two pieces of timber (100 x 50mm/4 x 2in) positioned over the plates on each side of the chassis in the engine bay.

It's now necessary to set the engine gearbox unit at approximately the correct level within the chassis so that engine and gearbox mounts can be correctly set (see the accompanying dimensional drawings on page 105).

When you're happy with the position of the engine, drill a 12mm/0.472in hole (this is big enough to allow some movement for adjustment) through the engine steel mounts, through the timber, and through the steel plates on the chassis.

Now lift the engine and remove the pieces of timber and substitute proper rubber engine mounts. If you're fitting a 'Pinto' SOHC engine from the Sierra and have used the appropriate drawing dimensions for the steel mounts, you can use a rubber mount 50mm (1.96in) thick on the right-hand side and a rubber mount 40mm (1.57in) thick on the left-hand side: the round type being the best fit. Tiger uses 5mm spacers under these mounts on some fitments. Only the centre rubber part of the standard Sierra gearbox mount is used, so you'll need to drill through the two rivets holding it to the shaped steel pan.

As a general guide to various engine installations see the accompanying photos.

Right-hand side Tiger Avon/'Pinto' engine mount pictured from rear of car.

Left-hand side Tiger Avon/'Pinto' engine mount pictured from the front.

OIL FILLER MODIFICATION (FORD SOHC 'PINTO' ENGINE)

Due to the height of the standard Ford SOHC 'Pinto' engine, the filler neck on the camshaft cover might need to be modified (see Drg 8.19 on page 111) so that it doesn't contact the underside of the bonnet (hood).

1

2

3

4

5

1. Engine fitted into position, resting on small wooden blocks. Drill a 10mm hole through the mount, wood and chassis, then lift the engine slightly and replace the wood with rubber engine mounts.

2. Rubber engine mount fitted between the mount to the engine and the chassis.

3. The 1.6-litre engine positioned on wooden blocks.

4. A prototype Ford Sigma steel plate engine mount in the making; the design was created using a cardboard template. The engine is raised to provide the required sump clearance and the down stay steel tube is welded in place as its support.

5. A mount being developed on the other side of the Sigma engine.

Tiger R6 with 16v Ford Zetec engine (fitted with throttle body fuel-injection), from the induction side ...

... and from the exhaust side. Again, this engine and the fuel-injection could be used in the Tiger Avon.

Ford Zetec engine fitted to a Tiger Avon.

The Avon Zetec's bonnet is wider over the air filters.

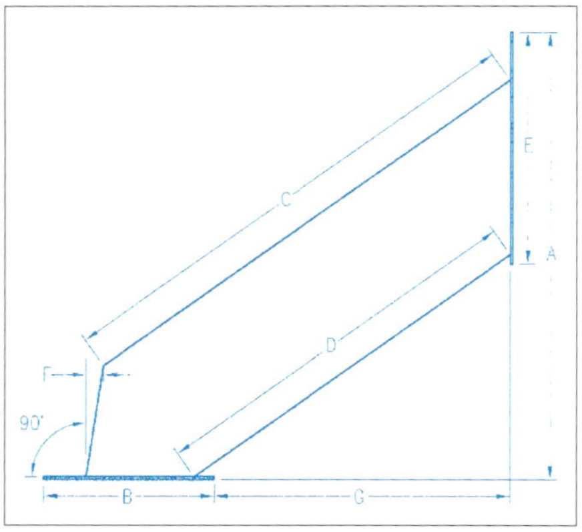

Drg 8.15a - Tiger Avon/'Pinto' SOHC engine mount (left-hand side) - front view. A = 180mm (7.08in). B = 65mm (2.55in). C = 190mm (7.48in). D = 140mm (5.51in). E = 85mm (3.34in). F = 10mm (0.39in). G = 115mm (4.52in).

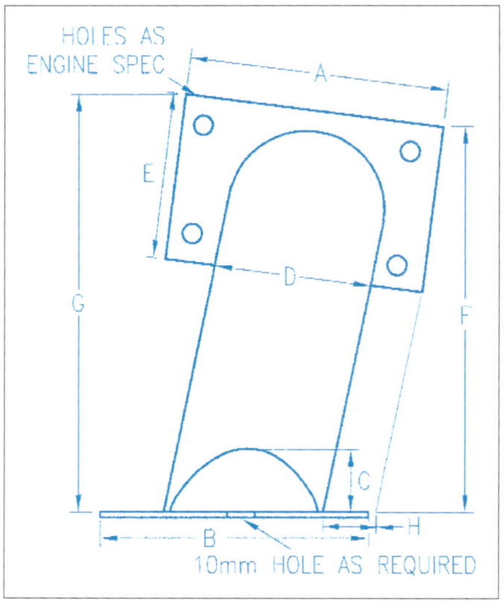

Drg 8.15b - Tiger Avon/'Pinto' SOHC engine mount (left-hand side) - side view. A = 90mm (3.54in). B = 90mm (3.54in). C = 35mm (1.33in). D = 16swg tube 50mm (1.96in). E = 85mm (3.34in). F = 165mm (6.49in). G = 180mm (7.08in). H = 10mm (0.39in). Plate = 3.2mm.

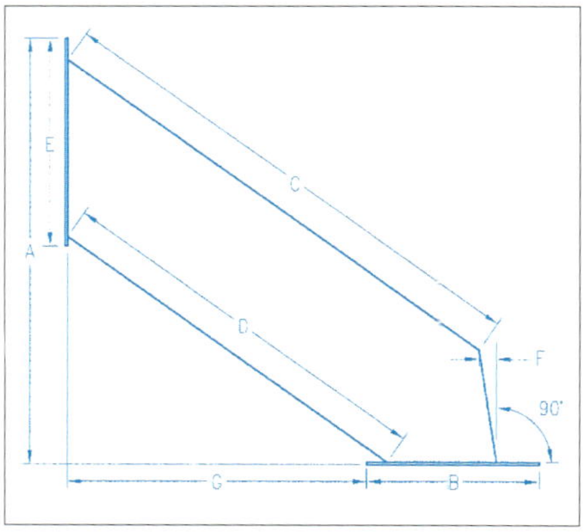

Drg 8.16a - Tiger Avon/'Pinto' SOHC engine mount (right-hand side) - front view. A = 140mm (5.51in). B = 65mm (2.55in). C = 145mm (5.70in). D = 100mm (3.93in). E = 85mm (3.34in). F = 10mm (0.39in). G = 90mm (3.54in).

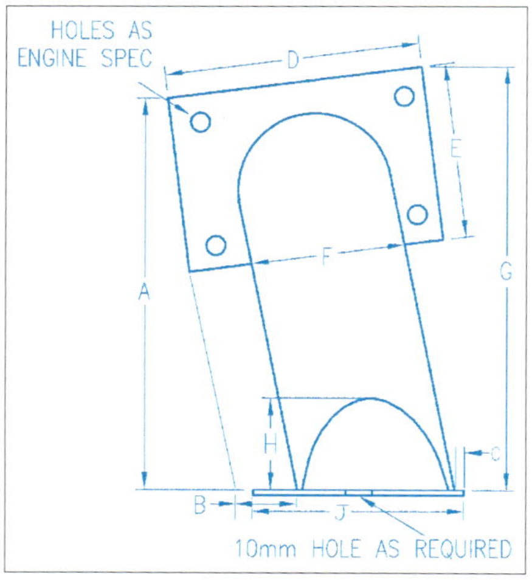

Drg 8.16b - Tiger Avon/'Pinto' SOHC engine mount (right-hand side) - side view. A = 130mm (5.11in). B = 20mm (0.78in). C = 10mm (0.39in). D = 90mm (3.54in). E = 85mm (3.34in). F = 16swg tube 50mm (1.96in). G = 140mm (5.51in) H = 35mm (1.37in). Plate = 3.2mm. J = 90mm (3.54in).

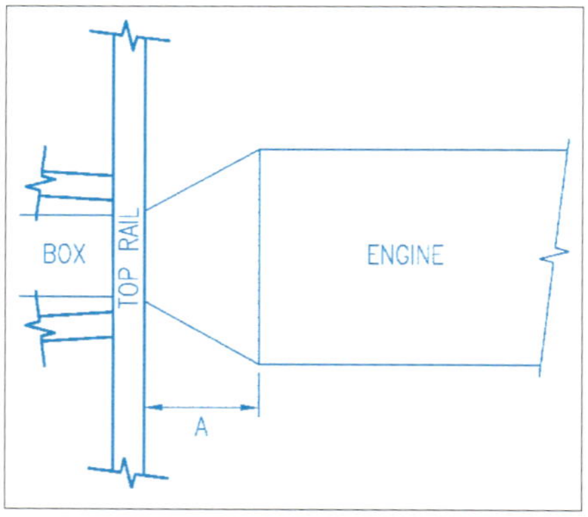

Drg 8.17 – Position of Ford SOHC 'Pinto' engine in relation to Tiger Avon top front chassis member. A = 200mm (7.87in).

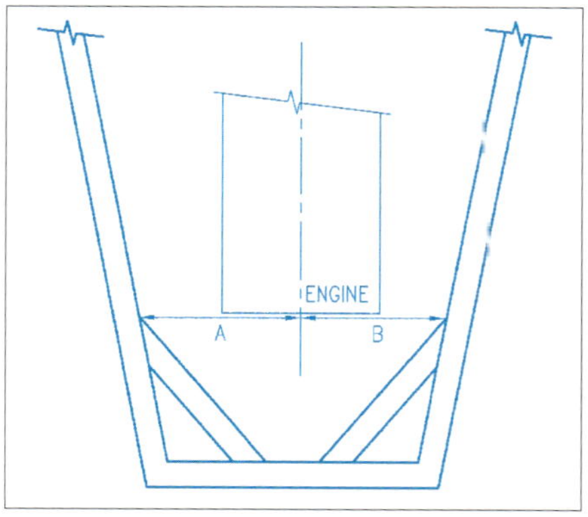

Drg 8.18 – Position of Ford SOHC 'Pinto' engine in relation to the centre of Tiger Avon chassis. A = 310mm (12.20in). B = 320mm (12.59in).

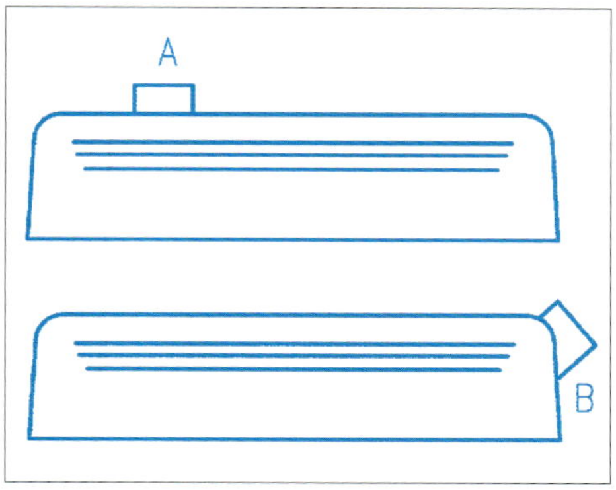

Drg 8.19 – Moving oil filler tube on Ford SOHC 'Pinto' engine. Remove existing filler tube at position 'A' and weld small plate over the resulting hole. Cut another hole of the same size in position 'B' and weld the filler tube at an angle over the new opening.

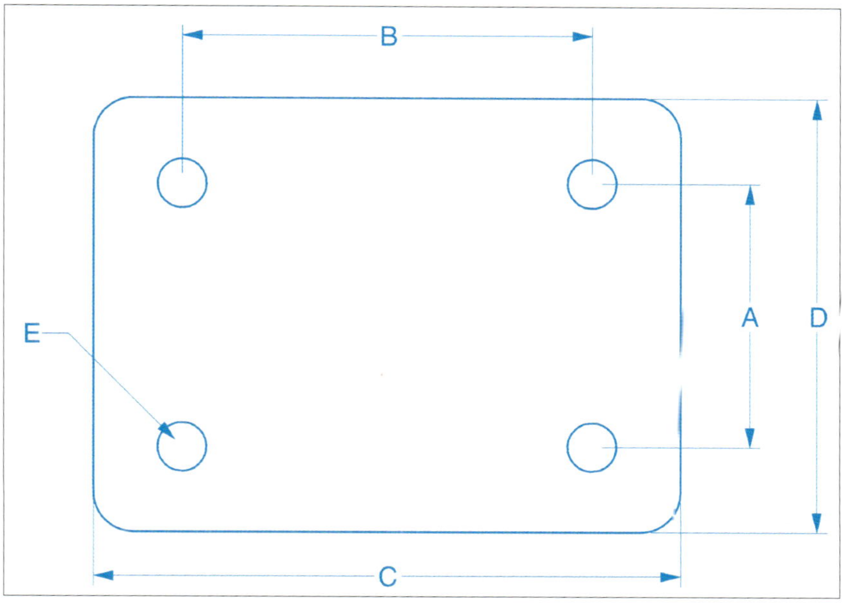

Drg 8.20 – Nearside left-hand Zetec engine plate. Material 6mm flat steel.
A = 55mm (2.16in)
B = 85mm (3.34in)
C = 125mm (4.92in)
D = 92mm (3.62in)
E = 12mm (0.47in)

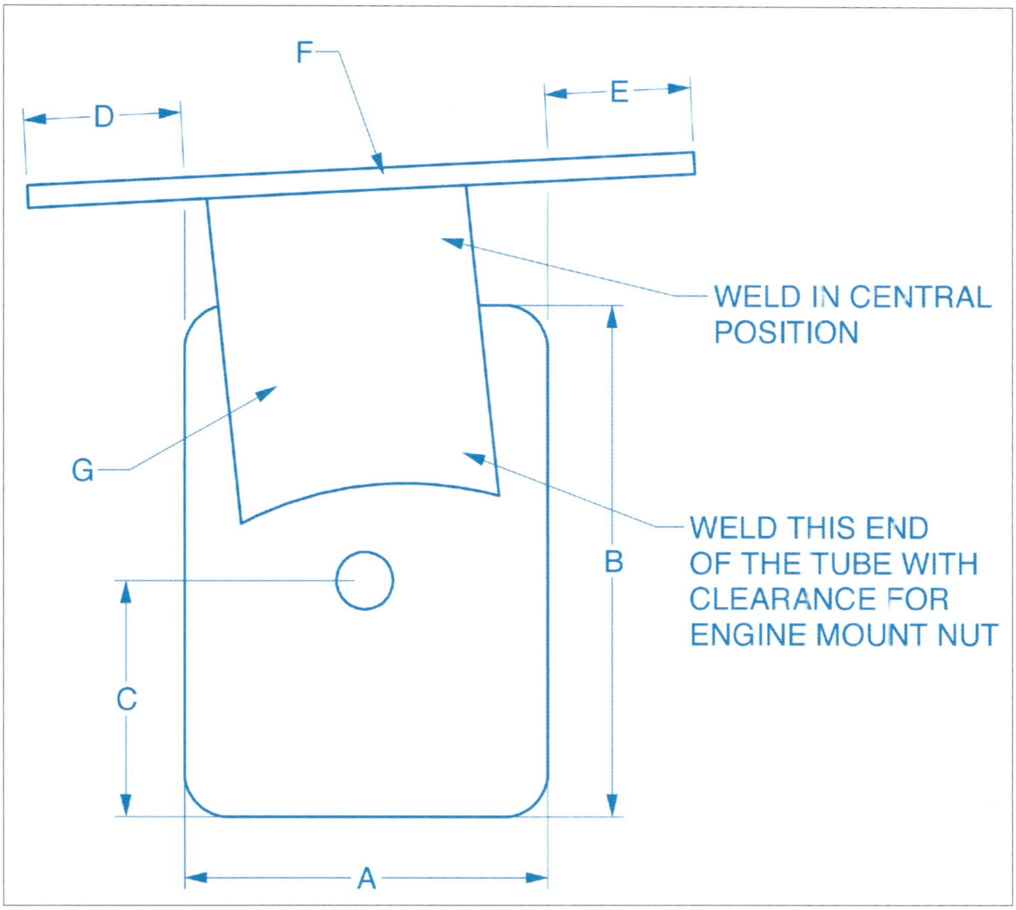

Drg 8.21 – Nearside left-hand Zetec engine mount.
A = 70mm (2.75in)
B = 95mm (3.74in)
C = 43mm (1.69in)
D = 30mm (1.18in)
E = 28mm (1.10in)
F = Drg 8.20 engine plate
G = 50mm dia tube

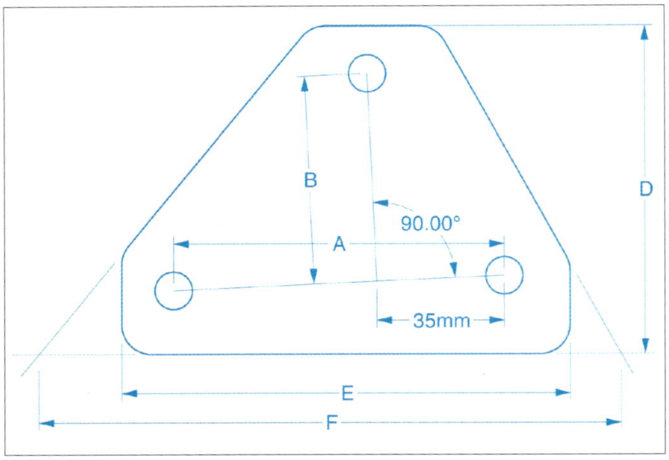

Drg 8.22 – Offside right-hand Zetec engine plate.
A = 94mm (3.70in) B = 58mm (2.28in) D = 92mm (3.62in) E = 126mm (4.96in) F = 163mm (6.41in)

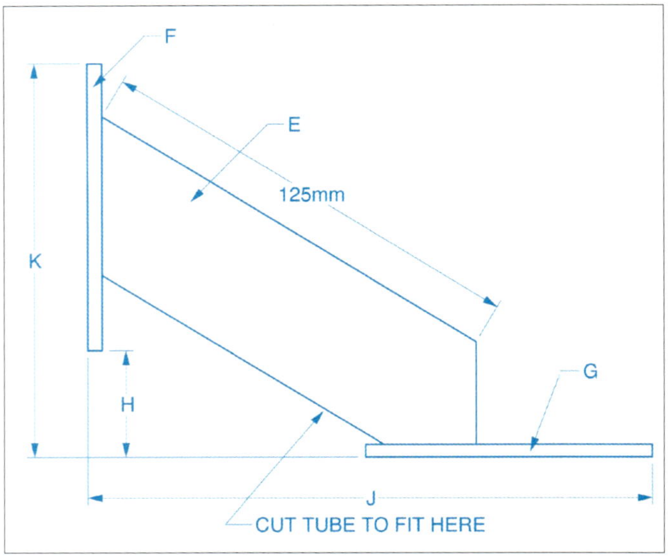

Drg 8.24 – Offside right-hand Zetec engine mount.
E = 50mm dia tube F = Drg 8.22 engine plate G = 92mm (3.62in) H = 45mm (1.77in) J = 180mm (7.08in) K = 125mm (4.92in)

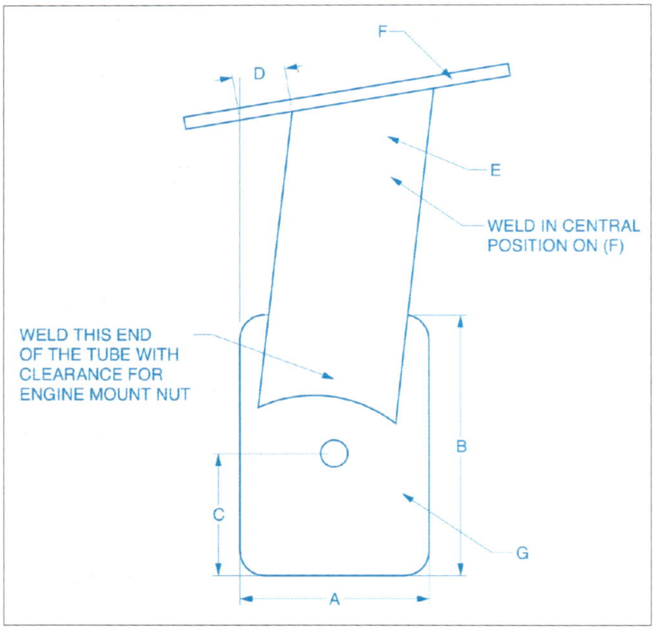

Drg 8.25 – Offside right-hand Zetec engine mount.
A = 70mm (2.75in) B = 95mm (3.74in) C = 43mm (1.69in) D = 20mm (0.78in) E = 50mm dia tube F = Drg 8.22 engine plate

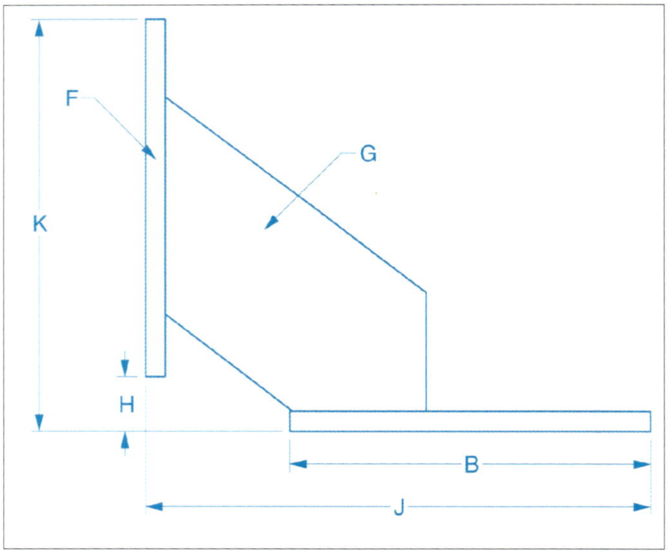

Drg 8.26 – Nearside left-hand Zetec engine mount.
B = 95mm (3.74in) H = 25mm (0.98in) F = Drg 8.20 engine plate G = 50mm dia tube K = 100mm (3.93in) J = 120mm (4.72in)

Tiger Super Six with Ford SOHC 'Pinto' engine (fitted with sidedraught carburettors). This is a popular combination for the Tiger Avon, too.

Electronic speedometer sensor fitted to diff drive flange (on a Tiger R6).

New lowline alloy sump for Ford Zetec. Note the raised front edge.

This Ford 'Pinto' SOHC engine sump (oil pan) has been reduced in height and an extra box added to the side to help restore lost oil capacity.

SUMP (OIL PAN) MODIFICATION (FORD SOHC 'PINTO' ENGINE)

The sump on most small specialist sports cars will usually need to be reduced in height by 40-45mm (1.56-1.77in). This will make the sump base approximately level with the bottom of the bellhousing (Sierra Type 9 gearbox). Certainly most SOHC and Zetec engines will need this modification. **Caution!** Remember that the pick-up pipe will need to be shortened by an equivalent amount and, ideally, you want a clearance of between 5 and 8mm (0.2 and 0.315in) between the pick-up and the sump base. You can check the clearance by placing Plasticine on the pick-up and temporarily refitting the sump (with gasket). Measure the compressed Plasticine to gauge the actual clearance. Zetec engines usually have alloy sumps fitted and are very difficult for the home builder to modify. It is recommended that a new, shorter alloy sump is purchased from Tiger or from Raceline Components.

PROPELLER SHAFT (DRIVESHAFT)

A modified propshaft will be needed which will be much shorter than the original Sierra one and which will have no central bearing (see drawing 8.27).

Warning! The Sierra propshaft must only be modified and balanced by a qualified engineer. Alternatively, you can buy a brand new propshaft (balanced for 120mph performance) from Tiger.

If you're fitting an electronic speedometer, a sensor disc will usually need to be fitted between the differential drive flange and the propshaft. Alternatively, a system using twin magnets can be used, the magnets being fitted to the propshaft. The sensor itself can be mounted on a made up bracket and should point directly at the holes in disc.

REMOTE GEARCHANGE (GEARSHIFT) LEVER

If you're fitting a remote gearchange lever mechanism, the first thing you need to do is remove the small piece of steel used as a reverse stop in the Ford Sierra gearbox (see illustration).

The modified gearlever (the standard Sierra item shortened and with a small piece of flat steel welded to it – see illustration) is secured in place by three M8 x 25 bolts.

The remote gearlever pivots in a

Left-hand drive Tiger Cat with Ford SOHC 'Pinto' engine (fitted with sidedraught carburettors).

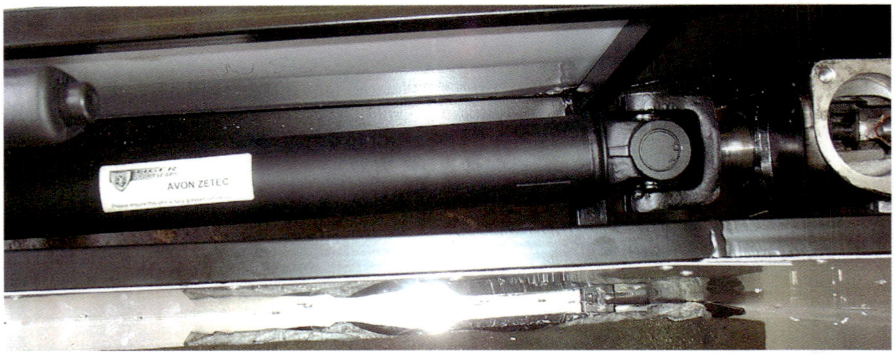

New Tiger Avon propeller shaft. Note the distance on the sliding part of the prop, between the oil seal and the U/J: this is to allow for movement of engine and gearbox mountings.

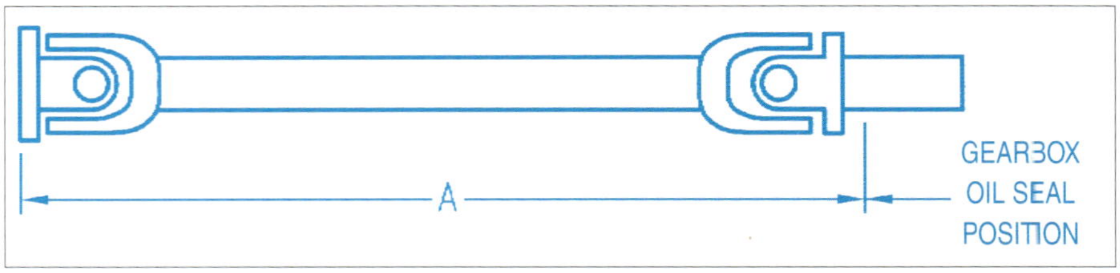

Drg 8.27 – Tiger Avon modified propeller shaft (driveshaft) dimensions. A = 650mm (25.59in). Total length 740mm (29.13in).

The Sierra gearbox reverse stop has to be removed when the 'box is operated by a remote gearlever.

Original Sierra gearlever modified for use with remote system.

Remote gearlever and complete linkage viewed from the side. Note that the strap bolts must be just loose enough to allow free movement.

Remote gearlever viewed from the rear (note reverse stop device).

Close up detail of gearlever reverse stop mechanism.

Rose joint attached to the chassis and is attached to the original lever by two steel straps (see illustration).

The new reverse stop is now the adjustable bolt on the right-hand side of the gearlever support bracket (see illustration). Reverse is found by pushing down the remote gearlever so that it clears the reverse stop. Alternately, a complete new 'one-piece' remote assembly can be purchased and fitted directly to the existing type 9 gearbox (contact Tiger for more information).

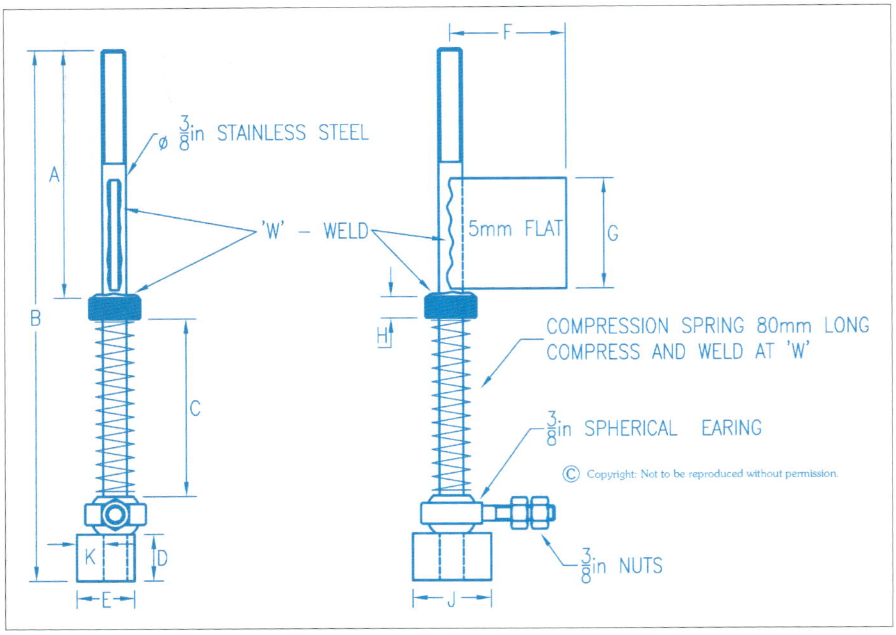

Drg 8.28 – Details of remote gearchange (gearshift) lever.
A = 110mm (4.33in). B = 210mm (8.26in).
C = 60mm (2.36in). D = 20mm (0.78in).
E = 15mm (0.59in). F = 40mm (1.57in).
G = 45mm (1.77in). H = 5mm (0.196in).
J = 25mm (0.98in). K = 6mm (0.23in).

Construction detail

The modified Sierra gearlever and the new remote gearlever need to be linked together. This is done with two pieces of 25mm x 5mm flat section steel, one each side.

Drill 8mm holes in the steel straps to take the securing/pivot bolts. Secure the straps to both gearlevers using two M8 x 35 bolts (grease all joints before fitting the bolts) which should initially be tightened and then undone slightly to allow the levers to move but without excessive freeplay (lash). Use locknuts to preserve the setting.

The reverse stop bolt fits through the hole in the bracket on the right-hand side of the transmission tunnel next to the gearlever mount. The bolt is locked to the bracket by two nuts, its head acting as the reverse stop. Reverse cannot be selected without pushing down the remote gearlever against spring pressure: this action moves the base of the gearlever clear of the stop.

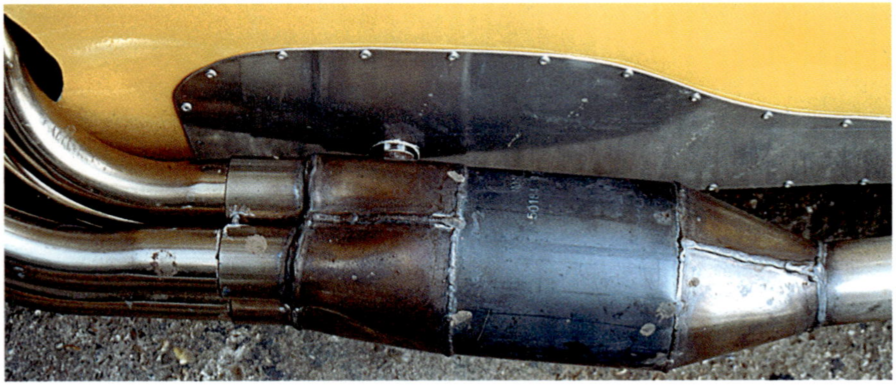

A Tiger R6 fitted with a catalysed exhaust system.

EXHAUST FRONT PIPES (GENERAL)

Tiger can supply stainless steel exhaust system components for Ford 'Pinto' SOHC and Ford Zetec-engined Tiger Avons.

Although the specific information in this section relates to a Ford SOHC 'Pinto' engined car, the general procedure is much the same for most applications. Remember, if you're fitting an engine manufactured after August 1995, it will need to be used with a catalysed exhaust system and, probably, fuel-injection to meet emission requirements.

The exhaust downpipes (headers) will need to exit the engine compartment via a hole in the side of the body. You need to work out where the exit hole will be and initially make a hole in the centre of this area with something like a 50mm (2in) hole cutter. You can then enlarge the hole, check fitting each pipe as you go. **Important!** Make sure you leave enough clearance between pipes and body opening to allow for engine movement.

Secure the downpipes to the cylinder head but leave bolts loose.

With felt tip pen or pencil mark the downpipes to show how far they should engage with the 4 into 1 collector when it is correctly fitted. Apply exhaust sealer to the pipe ends.

Push the collector on to the ends of the downpipes, using a piece of wood to drive it on until the marks you made are just covered. Now a 3.2mm (0.125in) hole can be drilled in the

Two rubber mounts to support the silencer bracket. Use large ('penny') washers on the inside of the body to support these mounts.

The silencer bracket fixed to the flexible mounts.

Typical complete exhaust system.

underside of the collector and into one of the downpipes, and a self-tapping screw inserted to lock pipes and collector together. Some exhaust manufacturers incorporate small pieces of tube on the underside of collector and downpipe which act as 'eyes' so that you can use a nut and bolt to secure the pipe joint.

Silencer

Using a hacksaw, cut a slot in the 2in diameter open end of the silencer to enable the exhaust bracket to clamp the silencer to collector.

You may need to shorten the 2in diameter pipe from the collector (they're usually too long) to obtain the correct length. Hold the silencer in its correct final position (keeping the tailpipe

Tiger 'one-piece' gear remote for Avon.

at least 38mm (1.5in) from the rear wheelarch) against the collector and mark where to cut the collector pipe.

Two small rubber mounts are used to secure the silencer bracket to the body (see illustration on page 117). Use large washers inside the bodywork to hold these mounts in place.

An exhaust clamp secures the silencer to the collector; place it in position and tighten. Tighten the bolts securing the downpipes to the cylinder head.

An early Tiger Avon with clamshell-type front wings (fenders).

BLEEDING BRAKE HYDRAULIC SYSTEM

Ususally, you'll need an assistant to help carry out this procedure. **Warning!** Ensure **all** brake pipe connections are tight and that all hydraulic pipes are properly supported.

Fill the brake fluid reservoir with fresh brake fluid.

Pour a small amount of brake fluid into a glass container and place one end of the bleed tube into it, ensuring it remains below the fluid level. Connect the other end of the tube to one of the front calliper bleed nipples.

Open bleed nipple and gently pump the brake pedal four or five times, then tighten the nipple. Check the brake fluid level in the master cylinder.

Repeat the procedure until there is no evidence of air escaping from the system (bubbles in the bleed tube).

Use the same procedure for all four brakes (fronts first, then rears) making sure the master cylinder reservoir is never allowed to empty.

The brake pedal should now be in a normal position when at rest and have a 'hard' feeling very soon after you begin to press it. **Warning!** If the pedal has a 'spongy' feeling and only becomes harder if you pump it, there is still air trapped in the system which **must** be bled out.

Cycle wing (fender) support brackets on a Tiger Cat.

A pedal that sits low and needs one or two pumps before it feels better usually indicates that the rear drum brakes (if applicable) need adjustment.

CLAMSHELL-TYPE WINGS (FENDERS)

Long clamshell-type front wings can be fitted if preferred. They'll need to be bolted through the side of the bodywork using 'penny' (large) washers on the inside of the GRP to spread the load. The front of each wing is supported by a bracket which is usually bolted to the headlamp supports.

These cycle wings have rubber edging fitted to meet IVA requirements.

Avon Tiger-manufactured racing alloy radiator sits on two steel brackets.

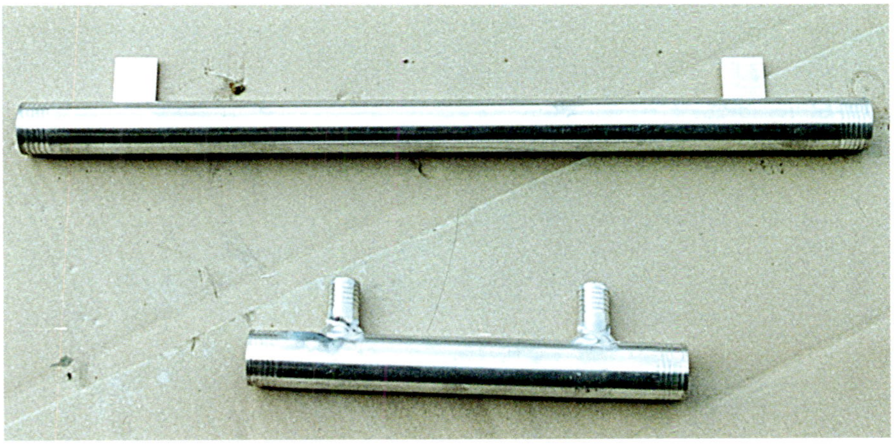

Alloy coolant tubes for the Ford Zetec engine.

CYCLE-TYPE WINGS (FENDERS)

Cycle-type wings are the usual choice because you can buy them off the shelf or you can adapt trailer wings which, again, are readily available. Cycle wings are attached by made up brackets fixed to the front uprights.

It's important to set the front wheel camber *before* fitting cycle wings.

ENGINE COOLING SYSTEM

Radiator

The radiator sits at the front of the chassis. Lower brackets, attached to the bottom chassis rail, can easily be made for various sizes of radiator. Sit the radiator on the bottom brackets and lean it against the top chassis rail (usually with a small piece of rubber interposed). A bracket, bent to give the correct fit, and bolted to the chassis, secures the radiator at the top.

Hoses

The top hose runs from the top of the radiator to the thermostat housing on the engine, while the bottom hose runs from the bottom of the radiator to the water pump.

If you're using an engine with an extra small outlet from the thermostat (about 8mm), this goes up to the small outlet on the expansion tank. If there is no extra outlet on thermostat block, the small outlet on the expansion tank needs to be blocked.

It's advisable to have an air bleed device in the top of the radiator. If the header tank is made of metal, you can drill a suitably sized hole in the top of the rad and solder on a small nut to take a 5mm (0.2in) or similarly sized bleed screw. Some radiators with plastic header tanks might already have an air bleed device.

On Ford Zetec engines, an alloy tube (top rail) is used for 'top' water and a 'twin pipe' alloy tube is used for 'bottom' water (see photo above).

Expansion tank

The expansion tank (see photo) is fitted in a high position just under the bonnet (hood) line. The large outlet on the bottom of the expansion tank connects to the bottom of the radiator and the smaller one, near the filler, goes to the engine's thermostat housing, if fitted. If the engine you're using does not have an additional small outlet on the thermostat housing, block the small outlet on the expansion tank.

If a heater is fitted, the outlet from the water pump goes to one side of the heater matrix, the other goes to the stub on the heated inlet manifold (Ford SOHC 'Pinto' engines).

Coolant expansion tank and mounting bracket.

CABLES

Throttle (accelerator) cable

For twin sidedraught carburettors you can make a cable stop bracket, or you can use an aftermarket one.

For a single downdraught carburettor a standard Sierra cable can be used after modification.

The outer cable stop on the chassis is drilled with a ⅛in (3.1mm) hole through which the inner cable passes. The throttle new pedal is drilled with two ⅛in (3.1mm) holes, the first in line with the outer cable stop, the second a little way below. The inner cable is passed through the 'in line' hole and back through the other and secured with a cable lock.

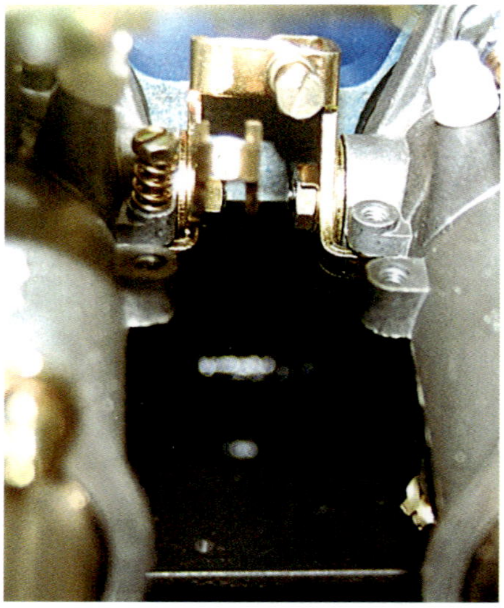

Small flat metal bracket attached beneath twin sidedraught carburettors to act as a cable stop.

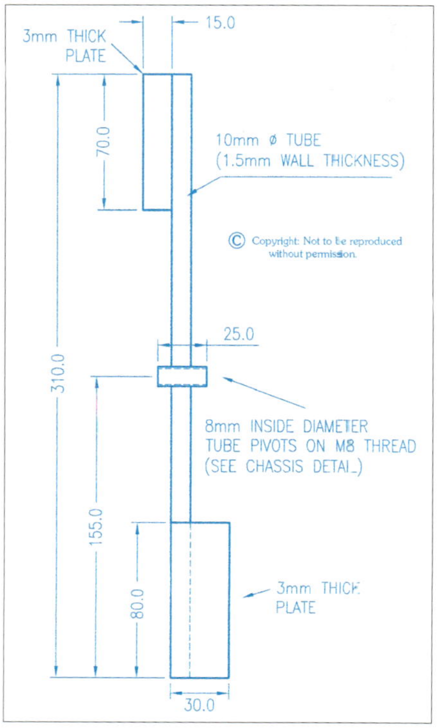

Drg 8.29 – Tiger Avon throttle (gas) pedal dimensions (millimetres).

Accelerator (gas) pedal

As the Sierra pedal cannot be used. The new pedal is made from a piece of 10mm thick wall round tube and 25mm x 5mm flat section steel (see the accompanying illustration).

Clutch cable

The standard Sierra clutch cable can be used on the Avon.

The ratchet system on the Sierra pedal is also used.

After passing the inner cable nipple through the hole in the release arm you can fit an 8mm short bolt through the hole to stop the cable nipple jumping out when you're driving.

Gearchange cable for sequential motorcycle gearbox

There are two ways to design the gearchange mechanism for cars with motorcycle engine/gearbox, one is with a push-pull cable, the other is by an arrangement of Rose jointed rods and brackets.

The push-pull cable system works well and is used on the Tiger B6. A bracket is fixed to the centre of the tunnel inside the car to act as an outer cable stop and another cable stop bracket is fixed in the engine bay above the position of the gearchange lever. The original motorcycle gearchange lever will need to be modified (probably a flat section welded to it). A new push and pull gearchange lever is made for the cockpit and mounted on the

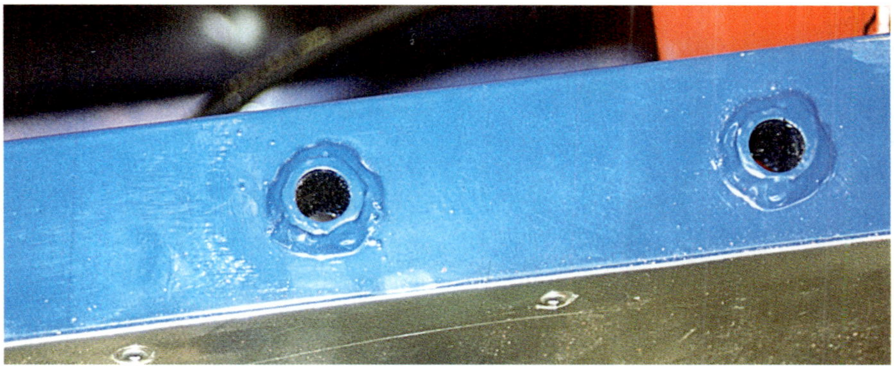

Seatbelt (four point 'racing harness' type) mounting points welded securely into the top rail of the chassis.

centre of the transmission tunnel in a comfortable position for the driver.

SEATS

You can use standard pad-type seats on your car or adjustable seats but, whichever type you choose, the IVA requirement is that they must be fixed securely and have a headrest.

If you're using adjustable seat runners, these must be bolted to the two chassis members under the seat; if using pad-type seats, brackets can be made to screw to the underside of the seat which, in turn, are bolted to the chassis members.

SEATBELTS

Single lap and diagonal seatbelts are no longer legal with the new IVA test. Four-point belts should be used; the top fixings on the top chassis rail, and the lower ones on the chassis each side of the seat.

The seatbelt must be marked to meet IVA requirements.

WINDSCREEN (WINDSHIELD)

You can use a small, low aero-screen or a full windscreen on your Avon. Whichever, check the IVA requirements

Windscreen (windshield) uprights will require a little twisting after fitting.

Windscreen upright support – measure 100mm from the edge of the bonnet to the first hole.

A completed windscreen (windshield). Note the stud fasteners in the frame for full weather equipment.

Mini-type wiper motor and drive to wheelboxes.

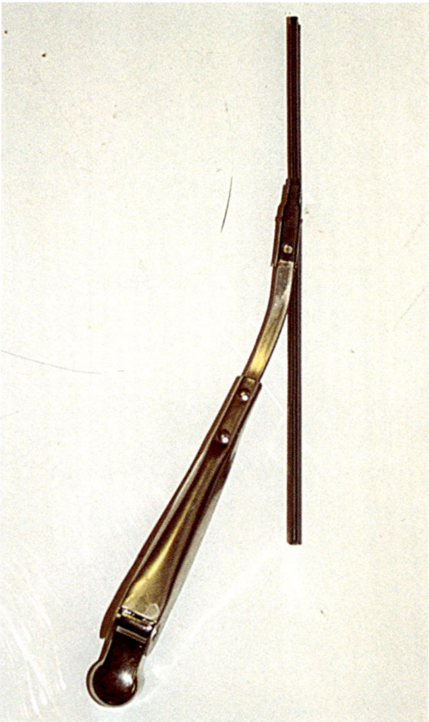

Shortened wiper arm with shortened blade.

regarding the safety glass (usually an 'E' marked windscreen is required, but an equivalent standard might be accepted).

The windscreen uprights can be made from flat alloy strips 5-6mm (0.2-0.24in) thick and 40mm (1.6in) wide (see photo) or you can use bespoke laser cut uprights.

The alloy channel for the frame is difficult to bend without special equipment, so it's probably easier to purchase one already bent from Tiger. If at some stage you're going to fit full weather equipment, it's worth drilling and pop riveting the fixing studs around the frame *before* you fit the glass into it.

If a full screen is not being fitted then there is no IVA requirement for a demisting system, wipers or washers.

It is possible to buy a heated full screen that will meet IVA requirements from Tiger.

When having your glass cut to a special size, make sure that it carries the correct safety marks for IVA.

WINDSCREEN WIPERS

The wiper motor can come from various sources, the main problem being the sweep of the blades, though the amount of sweep can be changed by altering the arm from the motor.

The most commonly used wiper system is the cable type taken from the Mini and various other British Leyland models. This system uses a cable and two wheelboxes, the wiper arms being attached to the wheelbox spindles. The advantage of this set-up is that it is very easy to shorten the cable and very easy to fit the wheel boxes in confined areas. Also, by turning the wheel boxes upside-down the sweep is reversed.

Remember that the wipers must self-park without obstructing the driver's field of vision.

If you're using the Mini wiper motor, it's possible to change the self-park position by turning the small plastic part on the large toothed wheel in the motor gearbox through 180 degrees.

HEATER

A heater can, within reason, be fitted anywhere you choose. The IVA requires

A VW Polo heater modified for Tiger use.

A GRP airbox for windscreen demisting made by Tiger and attached by body filler.

no sharp edges under the dashpanel and, if a windscreen is fitted, a demisting facility which can be run from the heater with appropriate vents, trunking and a blower.

Usually the heater is fitted under the bonnet in front of the dashpanel next to the battery and, with slight modification, various types of heaters (usually from hatchback cars) can be used.

BATTERY

The battery is fitted under the bonnet and in front of the bulkhead, usually in a central position.

The battery can be held securely by a small steel clamp made to fit over the lower flange of the battery and to bolt through the chassis member beneath.

The rear flange of the battery is held by an angled bracket riveted to the bulkhead.

WIRING & SWITCHES

If you're using the wiring loom diagram included in this book, the standard Ford Sierra light switch is not used (saw it off).

Four switches are used on the dashpanel (fascia): hazard warning, lights, rear fog, heater fan.

ALTERNATOR & DRIVEBELT

If the standard Ford SOHC 'Pinto' engine is being used, there'll be very

Middle: The author cutting out a windscreen demister vent.

Left: Finished demister vents are fed from beneath via an airbox.

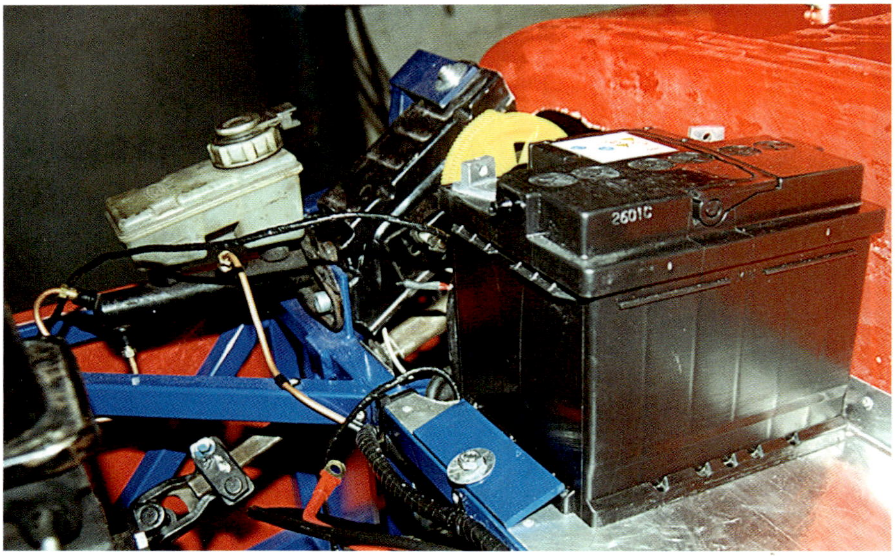

Battery in place and secured by a fabricated clamp.

Bracket to secure rear flange of battery.

little room on the right-hand side of the engine bay. Therefore a small alternator will be required (such as the Lucas LRA 101). It's likely that a small amount of the alternator's alloy casing will be required to be ground off (around the 8mm holes of the lower mountings and, possibly, from the edge nearest the right-hand side chassis). An 850mm (33.46in) alternator belt can be used with this arrangement: the standard Sierra alternator belt adjuster shortened to suit.

If you don't need it, saw off the standard Sierra light switch arm with a hacksaw.

The new carbon fibre dash.

Typical electric horn fitted to a Tiger Avon.

Lucas LRA 101 (or LRA 100) alternator in position, showing means of altering drivebelt tension.

A standard Ford Sierra rear view mirror fitted to a Tiger windscreen (windshield).

An external mirror fitted to the windscreen frame of a Tiger. Chrome mirrors can also be used. Check the radii of the mirror body for IVA compliance.

HORN

There are many types of electric horn you can use and all are easily fitted.

REAR VIEW MIRRORS

The standard Ford Sierra rear view mirror can be used in conjunction with a full windscreen.

SPARE WHEEL

If a spare wheel is going to be carried a mounting will need to be fixed to the rear chassis.

Rear lamps (round type).

Above & below: Weather equipment fitted.

Need Tiger's help?
E-mail – Jim@tigerracing.com

Chapter 9
Wiring diagrams

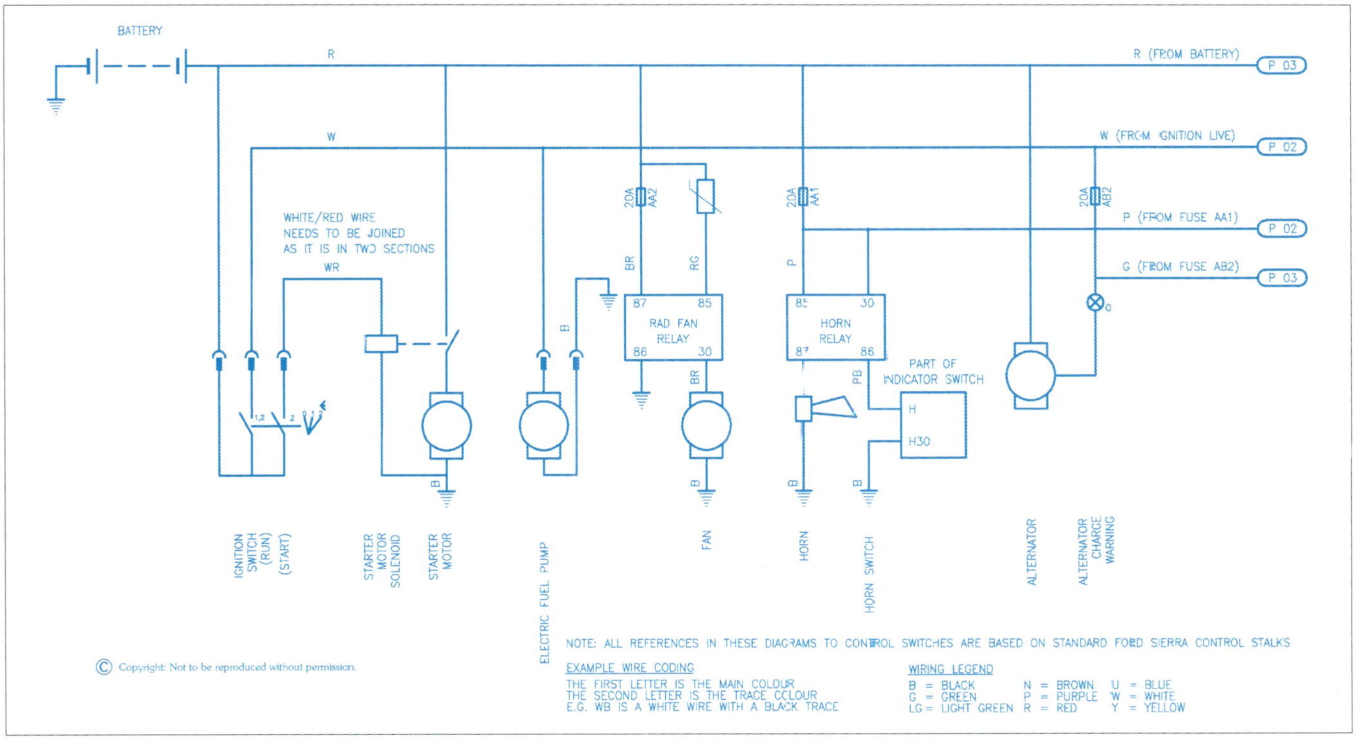

9.1 – Wiring diagram: Tiger Avon starting circuit.

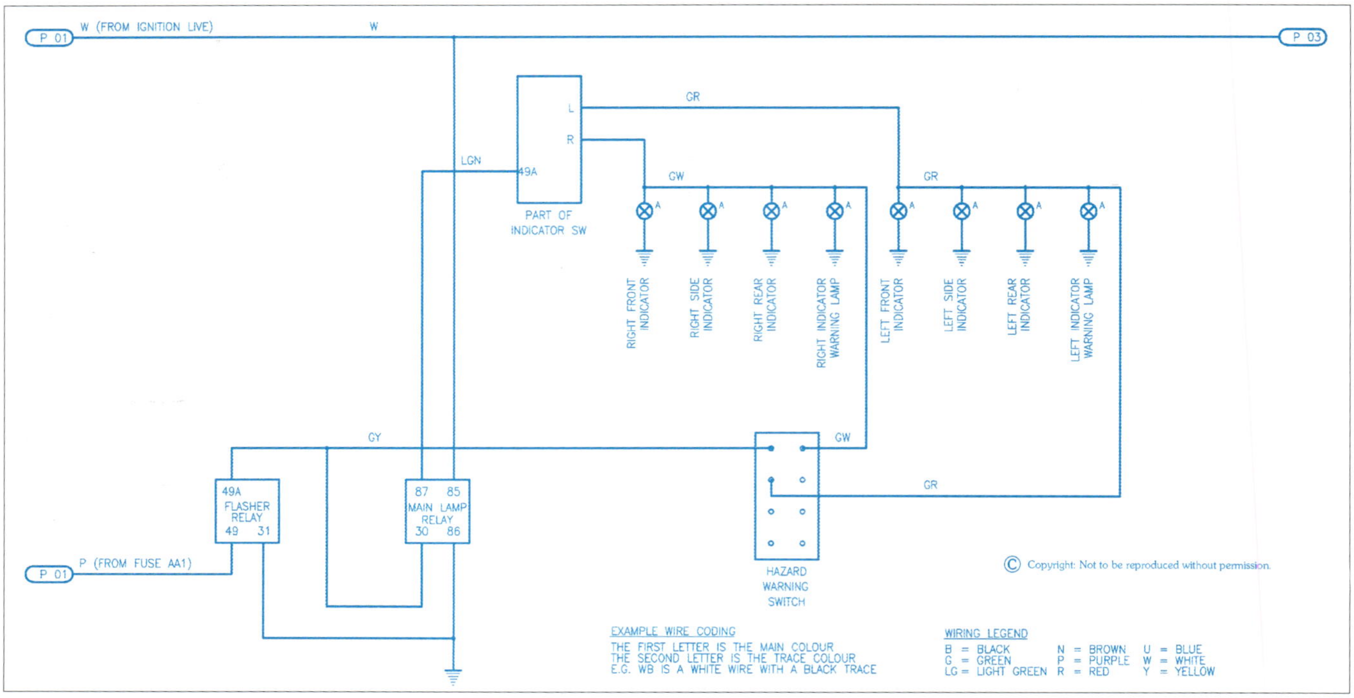

Above: 9.2 – Wiring diagram: Tiger Avon direction indicator circuit.

Below: 9.3 – Wiring diagram: Tiger Avon lighting circuit.

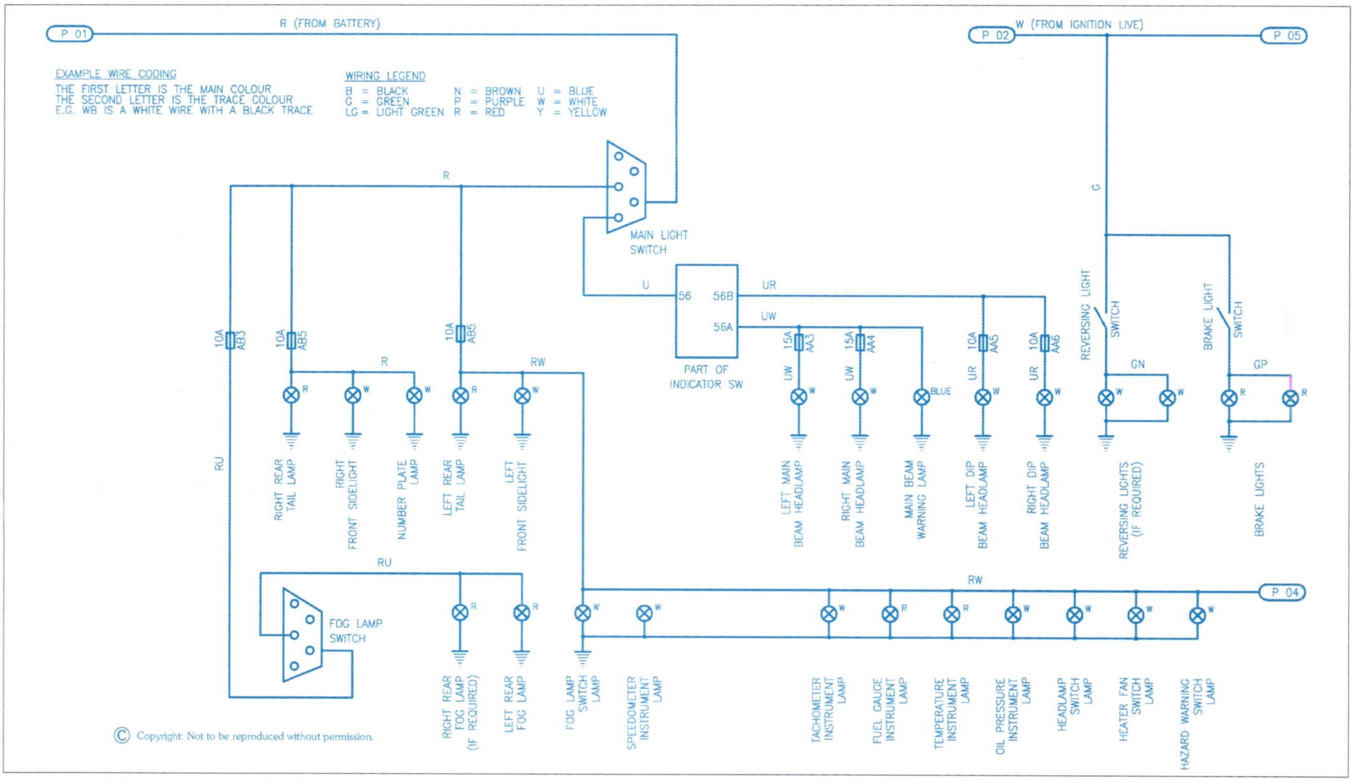

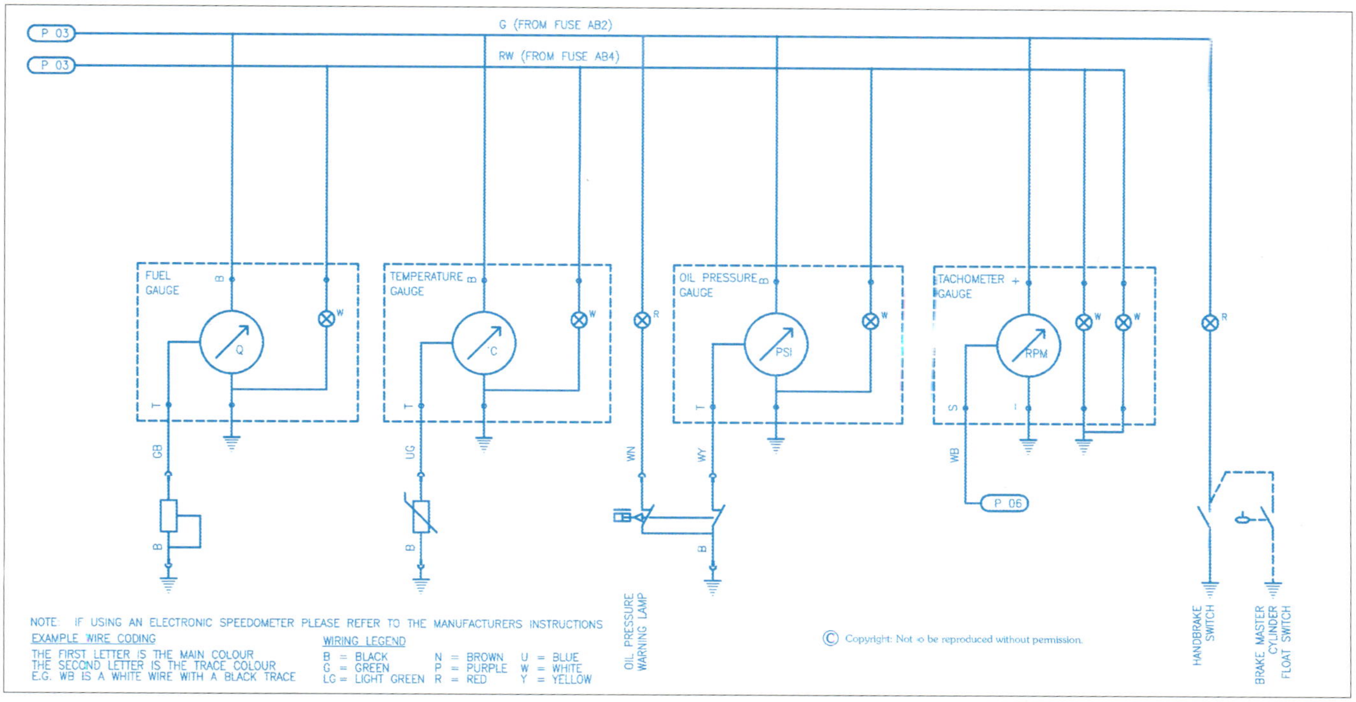

9.4 – Wiring diagram: Tiger Avon instrument circuit.

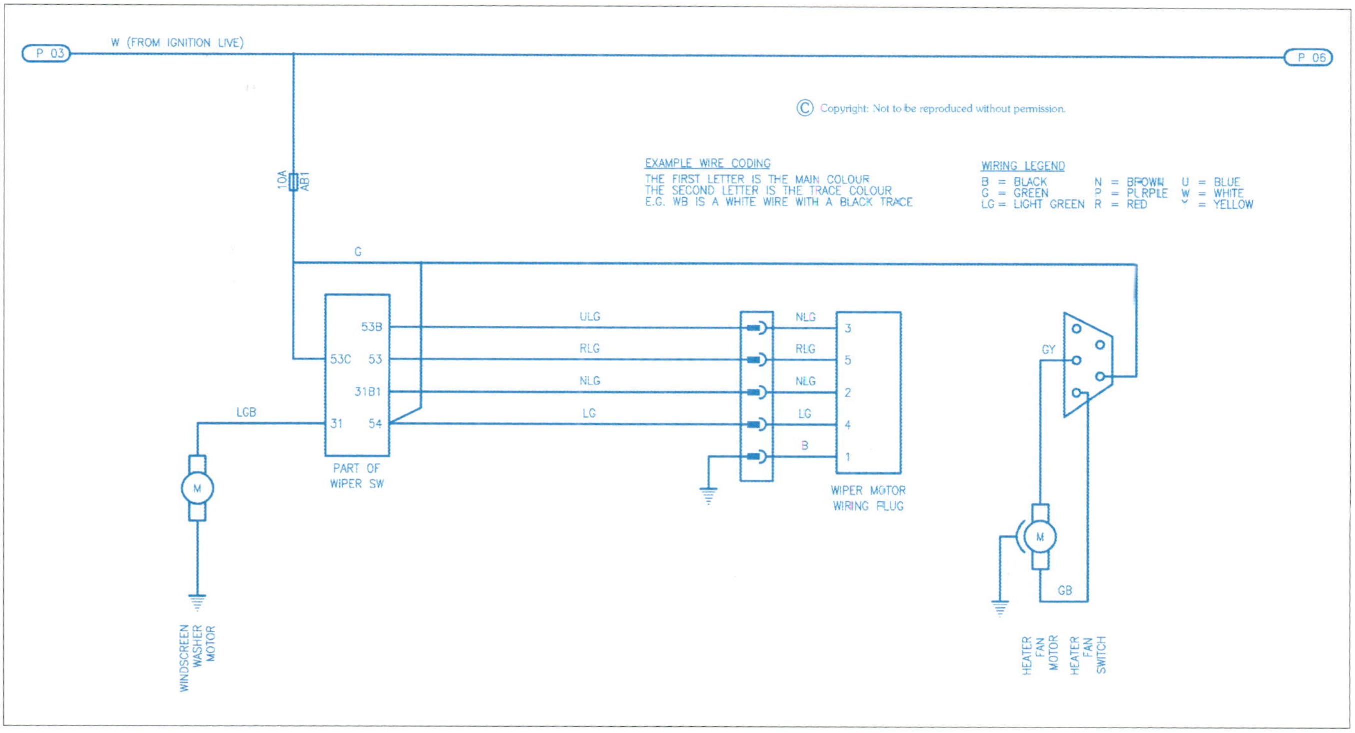

9.5 – Wiring diagram: Tiger Avon wiper and heater circuit.

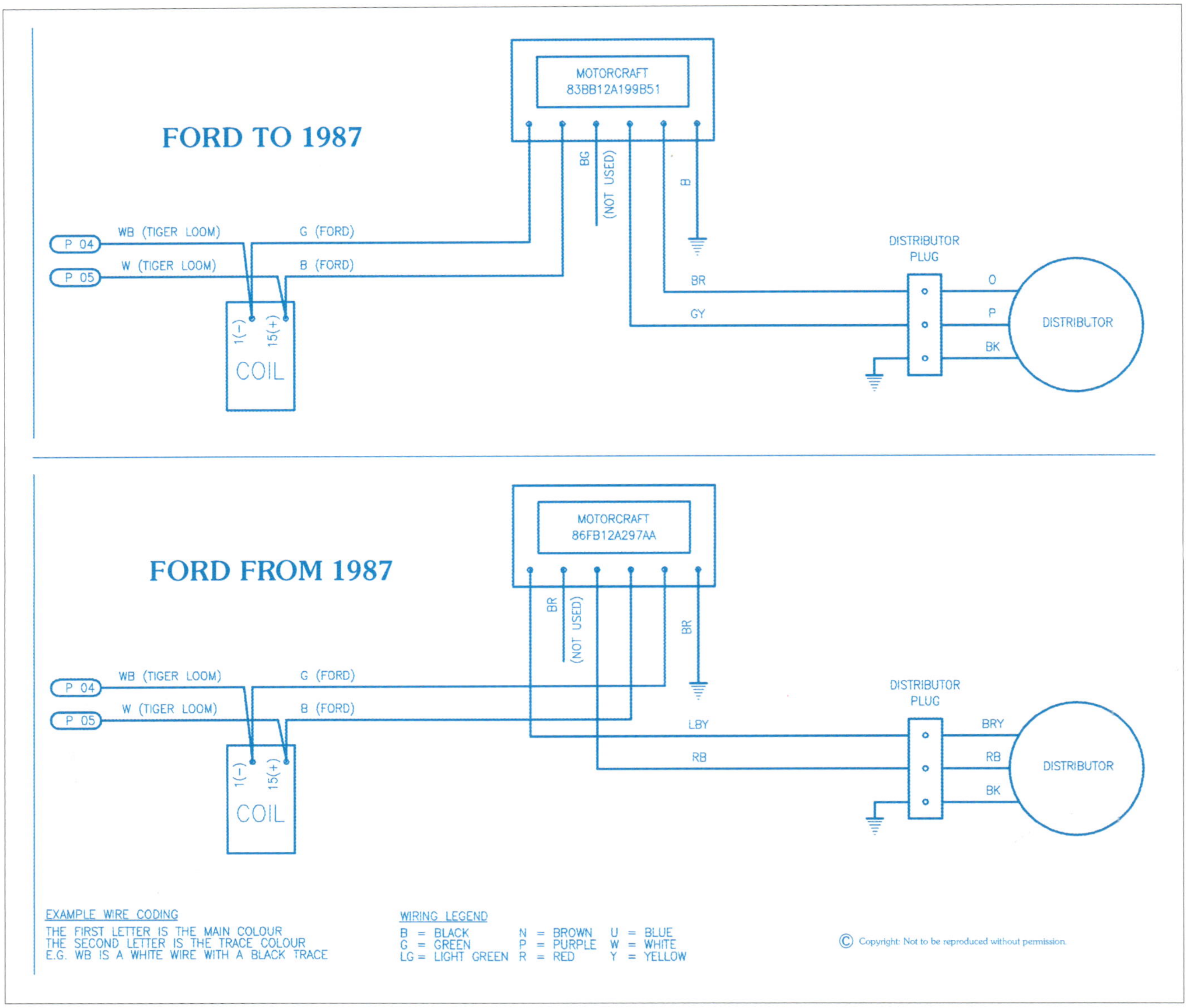

9.6 – Wiring diagram: Tiger Avon ignition circuit.

Chapter 10
Owning a Tiger

As you've worked your way through this book you'll no doubt have learnt that whatever your own level of mechanical aptitude a little effort, some imagination, and a chunk of dedication is all that's needed to take to the road in a car you've built yourself. Just imagine it! The open road, the sun shining, the wind in your hair ... it's a classic scenario and one which no doubt you've envisaged (go on, admit it!). But, in fact, Tiger motoring has much more to offer than just this simple idyll, and this chapter should give an insight into life with a Tiger after all the hard work's done. Defining what it means to own a Tiger is difficult to nail, but let's give it a try ...

One thing you'll definitely have picked up from this book is that your Tiger will be exactly that: *yours*. There are already hundreds of Tigers on the UK's roads (and a scattering throughout the rest of the world), and each is as individual as its owner. Whether distinguished by something as fundamental as an off-beat engine

Tiger events of all types are great places to meet ...

... like-minded enthusiasts and swap ideas.

You'll always find ways to individualise and improve *YOUR* Tiger: this one features an unusual paint scheme.

Taking to the road in a car you built yourself is hugely rewarding.

Long trips in your Tiger are to be relished: many owners make the journey to Le Mans.

choice, or just a novel solution to a minor build problem, each car is a reflection of the person who put the effort into its construction. That, for many, is one of the major attractions of Tiger ownership and, alone, makes the hours of building worthwhile. A look around any club gathering is evidence enough of this enthusiasm and individualism, and sharing ideas is a favourite pastime of many Tiger owners.

Sure, it's possible to follow this book to the letter and end up with an excellent car at the end. Indeed, that would be the most straightforward way of hitting the road in your Tiger. But most people, even those who set out with the intention of following the instructions to the letter, will find areas that they can't resist personalising and that's one of the great car-building pleasures. Alternatively, a halfway house, particularly for those on a tight budget, would be to complete a fairly standard car and modify things at a later date.

Which leads me neatly to the next point: never think for *one minute* that your Tiger will ever be finished. The stage at which your project becomes road legal and makes its maiden trip is nothing more than an (admittedly huge and justifiably celebrated) milestone in the build. It's the stage of the build at which you can start using the car and your sense of achievement will peak (more on that later), but you'll always go on improving your Tiger, taking it that stage further. Once you start using your car, you'll discover those areas which you want to change to make the car better suited to your personal needs. Oh, and you can justify those actions to your sensible side by telling it you're increasing the car's value.

Somewhere near the beginning of this chapter, I set a characteristic scene; the one about the open road, remember? Fast forward yourself to this stage of the build and see

Competitive events are a great way to enjoy the performance of your Tiger. This owner is about to leave the line at a sprint meeting ...

... while Tiger's Storm demonstrator enjoys a track day at Cadwell Park ...

... and here's a Tiger Super Six at another track day.

if you can forecast the feeling of contentedness, if not sheer smugness, at your achievement. Multiply the hypothetical satisfaction by about 10 and you're nearly there: the feeling's almost matchless. After all, you're driving a car you built yourself along the public highway. Allow yourself a smile at least ...

And you needn't limit yourself to your favourite local roads. Plenty of enthusiasts get some serious usage out of their cars and who can blame them? Visiting the annual 24-hour race at Le Mans in central France, for instance, is an annual pilgrimage for many Tiger owners. Other enthusiasts have used their cars for extensive European tours. After all, why take the plane? If you've got a great car the holiday starts as soon as you pull out of your own driveway. And if it's a car you've built yourself, pride enters the equation, too. It's just one of those things you've got to do *at least* once.

OK, so your Tiger's complete, you've put a thousand or so miles under the tyres and probably passed a couple of weekends improving your creation. Life's good, you've got a car you still actually *enjoy* polishing and the neighbours are still curious. No doubt you've probably attended the odd car show or other event, too, and are on first-name terms with other builders who understand why your project has very nearly become an obsession.

But the thing you really want to know now is how your car performs at the limits of its performance envelope. Certainly, you now feel familiar enough with the car to give it a try. You're just about to become acquainted with another aspect of Tiger ownership: the track day. And when you roll up at the paddock, you'll look just the part. You're driving a car that hasn't cost so much you've had to remortgage

Tigers at Zolder circuit in Belgium.

Sunday morning open road!

Tiger enjoying a track day.

A line of Tigers at a sprint meeting.

the house, while the running gear is all sourced from widely available production machinery and so spare part prices are more than reasonable. Yet your car still has supercar-humbling performance and, as you're about to learn, handling to match.

There's no doubting it: track days are big news these days and the car you've built, the very one that impressed all who have been passengers, the very one that took you to Europe, the very one that you enjoy so much on your favourite piece of road, is also an ideal tool in this environment. A spin-off from these events is timed competitions often held just for Tigers. Lighthearted in tone, these events are great fun and usually take the form of sprints or autotests. I'm almost tempted to repeat what I said earlier about trying these things at least once. Except once won't be enough ...

Hopefully, this chapter has served to highlight some of what you've got to look forward to after your car-building project. Speak to others out there who have already been through the process and they'll no doubt tell you of their own experiences which will differ from those here. However, the sense of achievement you get from the first trip, the pride in using a car you built yourself, and the enjoyment of taking part in track days and the like seem to be common threads amongst all self-builders.

By reading this book, you've taken the first step towards embarking on your own project. You'll no doubt want to research more into costs and so on, which is wise. But there must be a crunch time, a point at which you simply decide to turn your armchair enthusiasm into the real energy required to start your own project. And when you're driving along that utopian clear road on a sunny day, you'll have no regrets whatsoever.

Adam Wilkins
Tiger Owner's Club

TIGER PROJECTS AND SELF-BUILDER'S CARS

The cars pictured throughout this chapter illustrate the huge diversity of cars built by Tiger owners and by the Tiger company. These cars also demonstrate that by using the techniques described in this book and their own imagination, self-builders really can create the car of their dreams.

Early Avon fitted with clamshell wings (fenders).

Top & above: Tiger Cat.

Left & above: Formerly the GCS and now the Tiger Hawke.

Spanish Tiger with owners Martin & Bev.

First Ford 'Kent' 1600cc crossflow-engined race car.

Late Super Six (Ford 16v Zetec-engined).

2001 model Super Six ('Pinto' SOHC).

Tiger at Brands Hatch.

Super Six with automatic transmission and very luxurious interior.

Tiger Super Six used in the TV programme *Don't try this at home!*

Black looks good! Note the sidescreens for less wind at speed.

The Tiger R6 that was driven by touring car driver Jason Plato in the TV programme '*Mission Implausible*.'

Super Sixes, as featured in the TV programme *U-Bet*.

At the time of writing, this is the newest Avon, just completed by its owner. It's a road registered car with some track days in mind.

The first double bike-engined Tiger Z100 fitted with twin Kawasaki ZX9 engines ...

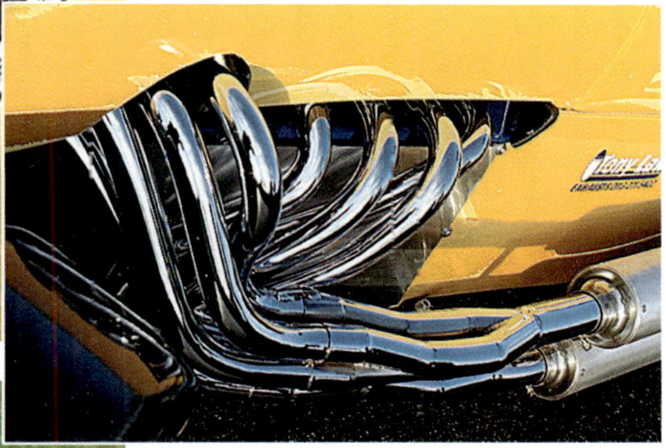

... Is there a faster accelerating (0-60mph) road legal sports car anywhere else in the world? ...

... This Z100 has recorded 0-60mph ...

... in 3.11 seconds!
(Tiger's 4wd Z100 has recorded a staggering 2.8 seconds!)

This Super Six took the full force of a head-on collision and the driver/builder is fine.

Tiger's new building and workshop facilities in Wisbech, Cambridgeshire, UK.

Author giving the new Tiger Aviator a spin.

Tiger's tribute to the D-Type.

Tiger Cub.

Tiger RS6 all-alloy.

Author's son, Paul's, R6. This was the fastest car throughout the 2009 season.

The new ZR6 supercharged alloy Tiger. This car has 278bhp and 211ft/lb torque @ 6500rpm.

Chapter 11
Racing your Tiger

There are race series run by various clubs for which you can enter your finished Tiger, and Tiger even holds its own race series at most of the major circuits in the UK. The 750 Motor Club runs various championships with a range of different classes which include car and bike-engined cars. Alternatively, hillclimbs and sprints are a good introduction to motorsport.

Full competition information sheets (including specifications) can be obtained from the 750 Motor Club (see appendix for address).

SUSPENSION & STEERING GEOMETRY SETTINGS

Optimising the suspension geometry on your Tiger for track use will require different settings to those generally used on public roads. **Warning!** If you have changed settings, even if it was just for a track day, don't forget to reset them for general road use.

Camber

Correct camber setting is very important for good handling. Though most builders seem to think of camber

Tigers competing at Lyden Circuit.

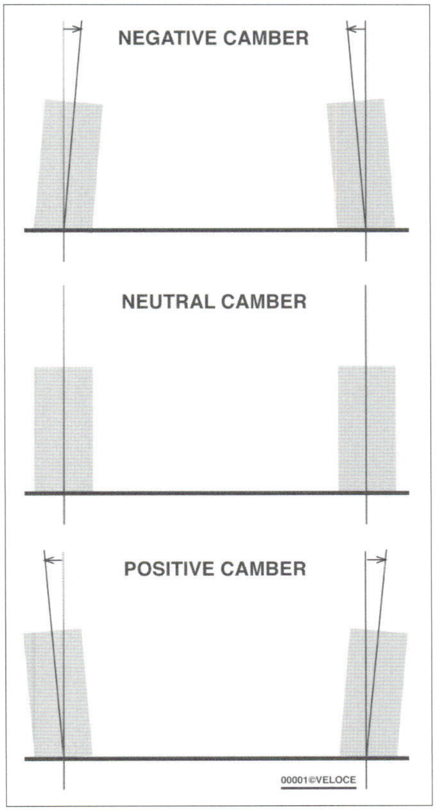

Drg 11.1 – Simple illustration of camber.

only in relation to the front wheels, it is equally important for the rear wheels.

Basically, camber is the amount (measured in degrees) that a wheel leans inward or outward in a vertical plane. When the top of the wheel tilts inwards, towards the car, camber is said to be 'negative' and when the wheel tilts outward away from the car it is said to be 'positive.'

As a guide for general road use and occasional track use, zero degree camber (which can be checked with a spirit level) is fine and will produce excellent handling characteristics. For circuit use, half to one degree of negative camber for both front wheels is a good starting point. You can then experiment with small changes to get the best handling for your individual car.

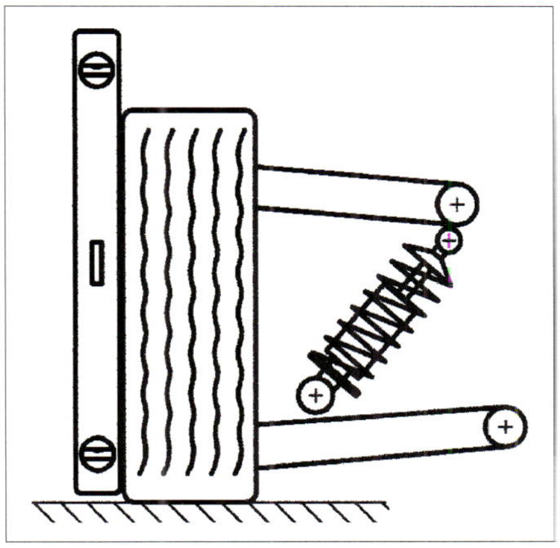

Drg 11.2 – A spirit level will indicate zero degrees of camber, but no other settings.

Castor

Castor angle provides stability and enables the steering to have some degree of self centring. Looking at the right-hand side of the car, with the front wheel to your right, imagine a line drawn vertically (at 90 degrees to the ground) through the centre of the wheel. Castor is produced by positioning the top ball joint behind (towards the rear of the car) this vertical line and the bottom ball joint in front (towards the front of the car) of the line. In general, caster is determined by how much the car weighs and for light cars, such as the Tiger Avon, between 4 and 6 degrees of caster is a good starting point to the process of determining optimum caster for an individual car.

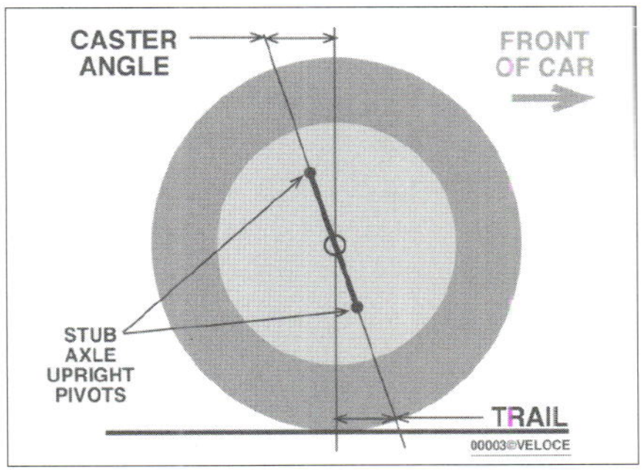

Drg 11.3 – Simple illustration of caster.

Bump steer

Bump steer describes the effect when uneven surfaces momentarily cause the car to steer to the right or left. Basically, suspension movement is creating unwanted steering movement because of steering geometry changes.

On the Tiger Avon most bump steer has been eliminated. If there is a problem, shimming the steering rack mounts up or down will normally solve it.

Tracking (toe)

For general road use Tiger Avon tracking is set at 3 to 4mm (1/8 to 3/16in) of toe in. 'Toe in' is when the fronts of a pair of wheels on the same axle are closer together than the rears (imagine the wheels as being pigeon-toed). As an example, if the distance between the rims of the front wheels (measured at hub height) is, say, 1500mm at the rear (behind the axle) and 1496mm at the front (in front of the axle), then toe-in equals 4mm.

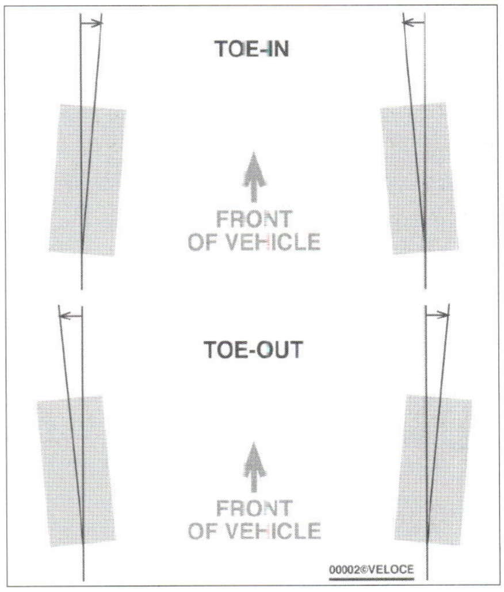

Drg 11.4 – Illustration of tracking (toe).

CORNER WEIGHTS

'Corner weights' are the individual loads carried by each of the four springs supporting your car.

To set the corner weights on your Tiger Avon you'll need a corner weight gauge and shock absorbers with adjustable spring platforms. Balancing your car's weight has great benefits for handling: the car will feel better when braking and cornering, and will generally be a better balanced and handling car.

The aim is to get the corner weights equal across axles and, if possible, at all four corners (the latter being more difficult to achieve) of the car. Don't forget when adjusting corner weights to put the correct weight in the driver's seat (equal to the normal driver's weight); also the tank should contain the amount of fuel you anticipate using over race distance. Remember, too, that relatively heavy things like radiator header tanks and battery can be positioned favourably in terms of weight distribution.

HANDLING

Your Tiger Avon will handle reasonably well 'out of the box,' providing all the main settings like tracking, camber and castor have been adjusted correctly. However, to optimise the handling of your individual car for racing, you'll have to go testing on a circuit.

You'll find that the difference between standard road tyres and racing tyres for the track will change the handling considerably, so the first consideration is which tyres to use. Go to a race meeting, check out what tyres the front runners are using and then buy the same.

Before going to your test session on the circuit, check camber, castor and tracking settings and take details of these settings with you.

Set cold tyre pressures correctly (starting at 20psi) and record the changes after a few laps when the tyres are warm. You can now try different suspension settings and tyre pressures, recording the resulting lap times until you feel you've found the best settings.

If changing camber settings, remember to check, and if necessary reset, the tracking afterwards.

Remember, uneven braking characteristics and an unbalanced car will heat the tyres unevenly, so a slight suspension setting change might also mean the requirement of a fine tune to brake balance.

A Superlight wheel fitted with Yokohama racing tyre (road legal).

YOUR RACE CAR

Here's a guide to basic requirements for your race car in the UK, of course other countries will have different requirements. Highly recommended is getting a copy of the MSA (Motor Sports Association) competitor's year book known as the 'blue book' which covers all racing regulations.

A trip to a race meeting and talking to competitors is recommended before you start racing. Tell the racers that you're just starting to race and ask their advice. Accept that when you start racing there is a steep learning curve to go through.

750 Motor Club

It's a very good idea to join the 750 Motor Club (which is not confined to 750cc cars) which will give you access to all relevant race regulations. You'll also need to be a member to race in their series.

BARC

It's a good idea to join a motor racing club. BARC run a lot of the Tiger races through the season, and you can find its address at the rear of this book in appendices/useful addresses.

Racing licence

You'll need an MSA race licence. To obtain one of these you will need to attend, and complete, an ARDS (Association of Racing Drivers School) course. You can attend these courses at most of the race circuits around the UK and when you have completed and passed the ARDS course you'll need a medical check-up by your GP (the form for the medical is on the rear of your MSA application form).

When you receive your licence, you'll also receive a copy of the 'blue book' which is the Bible of racing regulations.

Remember when building your car that it must be *capable* of passing an MoT test (though it doesn't actually need a certificate) if it is to be eligible to race in the 750 Motor Club series.

Tyres

Whichever tyres you choose, the compound will have to be listed as approved in MSA regulations. Tiger racing regulations state that the tyre compound must be the same on every Tiger entered. This is usually known as a 'controlled tyre,' and it makes for closer racing.

Engines

If you're building your Tiger to use on public roads but with motorsport in mind, then you must check the 750 Motor Club regulations for your chosen engine: it's very easy to make the engine 'illegal' through modifications. As an example, some classes let you fit larger carburettors, but in others the carburettor must remain standard with, maybe, jetting changes only.

Bores can usually only be overbored within defined limits, so it is important to check the regulations *before* you make any modifications to the engine. A list of Tiger regulations can be obtained from Laura at Tiger, for other championships contact the motor racing club direct.

Roll bar

Your standard Tiger Avon roll bar will need to be replaced because the minimum requirement for racing is one diagonal tube and two down tubes: all made from CDS tubing fixed to the

Full roll cage and four-point seat belts on a Tiger R6.

Another Tiger with full roll cage, fire extinguisher system and quick-release steering wheel.

chassis direct (welded or bolted, but if bolted 12.9 ton cap head bolts are recommended).

The roll bar will need a cushion-type pad fixed in the exact location of your racing helmet.

In the UK, check with the current 'Blue Book' for required roll bar specification. For Tiger races, it's a requirement that a full cage is fitted, as these are much safer than rear section only cages.

Fire extinguisher

A fire extinguisher is required. These are generally fitted in the passenger footwell, and must be of the correct size and MSA approved. Also, the extinguisher must be able to be operated by the driver from the driver's seat (usually via a cable system). The extinguisher system usually has two jets, one spraying into the driver's compartment, the other spraying onto the carburettor or fuel system of the engine.

Seatbelts

Racing harnesses are required and their threaded mountings must be welded to the chassis (you can see the correct positions on the chassis drawings). Alternatively, holes can be drilled through chassis sections, tube inserted and welded in place for maximum strength.

Foglamp (red light)

The rear of the car must have a very bright red light. This light is fitted centre rear and is intended for use in poor visibility (usually wet races).

Fuel filler & tank

The fuel filler neck must not be on the outside of the car. It cannot be within the driver or passenger compartment either. Most builders who intend racing their cars will put the filler neck above the tank and inside the body line. Most

Tiger Avon race car fitted with a full cage.

Full cage shown from above.

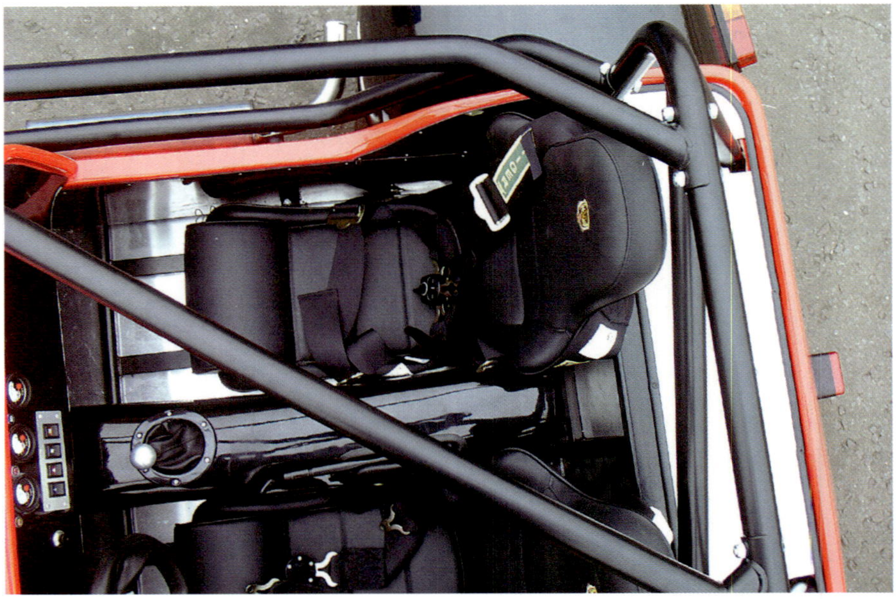

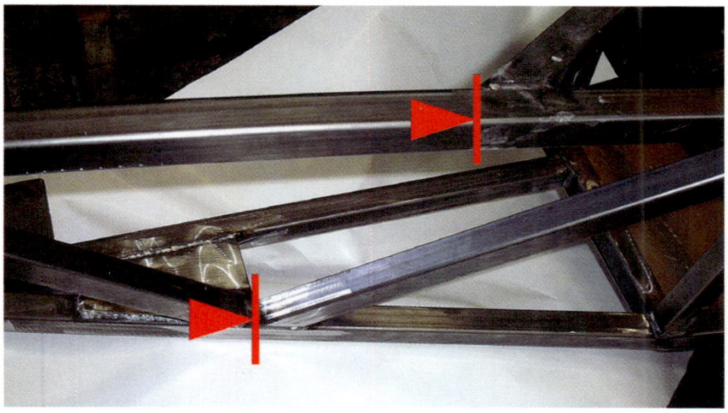

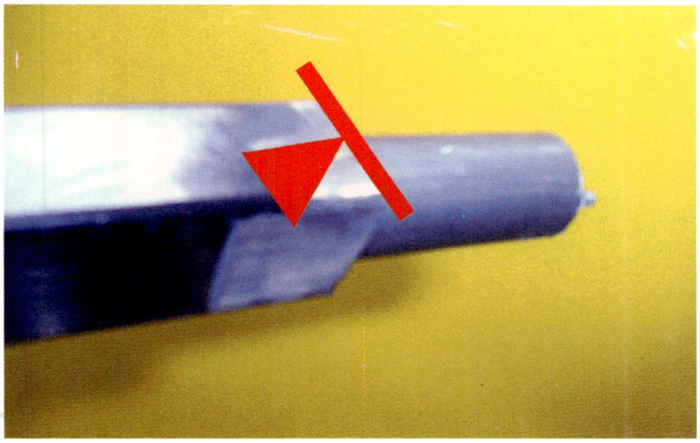

Repairing a race damaged chassis:
Top left: It is recommended to cut in both arrowed locations when removing a 'complete' front end damaged part of the chassis. Note that the top cut is next to the diagonal tube.

Above: New front end section fitted and welded while the gearbox remained in position. A tube used as a sleeve is knocked into the cut chassis

Left: A 16g tube is pushed into the cut chassis and the new front end chassis is slid over it. Leave a 2-3mm gap when aligned, to weld all three parts together (new front end – 16g tube – existing chassis).

Full Tiger grid.

race tanks use an alloy, screw-fitting filler cap in combination with a non-return valve in the tank breather system (this prevents fuel leakage if the car rolls). A standard road-type fuel tank is not suitable for racing.

Silverstone meeting.

Electrical

You'll require a means of isolating the engine electrical system. This is in the form of a battery cut-off switch which will also kill all other electrical circuits. If you have a fire extinguisher system that is operated by the battery, it must not be wired through the cut off switch. The cut-off switch is usually mounted under the roll bar on small clubman-type cars with no windscreen.

Tigers at Lydden in Kent.

Front running Tigers.

Silverstone winner, Paul.

Propshaft

Your car's propshaft turns at great speed so to protect the drive if it breaks or comes loose, a steel bar is required to be fitted inside the tunnel. This can be done in various ways, but we recommend 40 x 5mm flat section steel bar for this job.

Towing eye

It is required to weld or bolt a towing eye to the front and rear of your car. This is in case of breakdown on the circuit.

Engine oil

An oil catch tank must be fitted. It is connected to the oil breather pipes of the engine. Baffling will be required in the sump to prevent oil surge.

Exhaust system

The exhaust silencer must meet the noise limit for the circuit. Current noise limits are around 105 decibels and most standard silencers should be OK as they pass the IVA test at 101 decibels. The exhaust tailpipe is best kept inside the body line and should point downwards.

Rose joints

Quite a few 750 Motor Club racing series ban the use of Rose joints, so, as these joints are used on Tiger Avon suspension wishbones, check the regulations for the classes you wish to race in. Nylon bushes could be used in place of Rose joints if you need to comply with regulations for a particular class.

Generally you can use nylon bushes in place of rubber bushes if you want to 'stiffen up' your suspension.

Bulkhead

The bulkhead (between engine and driver/passenger compartment) must be sealed. The rear section housing the fuel tank must also be sealed off.

As mentioned before, all of the foregoing is intended as a guide. Check your 'blue book' for definitive current regulations.

MY FIRST RACING EXPERIENCE

So there I was, lining up on the grid in my Tiger Avon, the build of which was completed just the night before. Reading this book, you're probably in the midst of a build or planning to assemble a Tiger Avon right now. I was in exactly the same position when the single-marque Tiger Challenge race series was announced. It seemed rude not to up the spec of our Avon from track day car to racer and enter into the series.

As the car was not going to be registered for the road, the money saved on that process would go some way to covering the costs of the equipment demanded by Motor Sports Association (MSA) regulations. A roll cage, plumbed-in fire extinguisher and battery cut-off switch were all necessary additions. Even so, the Pinto-engined car came in under budget at less than £5000 all-up. Factor in the car-sharing deal amongst three of us, and it was a very cheap race car indeed.

The driver needed upgrading too – flame resistant overalls, a crash helmet, gloves and boots are all compulsory investments. You also need to attain a National B race license, which involves passing the ARDS test. While this seems nerve-wracking at the time, the reality is that it's much less demanding than the scrutiny you'll have been under to pass your road going driving test.

Admittedly, all of this is quite a chunk of expense all in one go. On-going costs then include race entry fees, tyres and fuel. Budgets vary wildly depending on the canniness and competitiveness of the individual, so it's worth asking around the paddock for drivers' views on the cost of a season's competition.

Thoughts of expenditure evaporate as soon as you wrap your gloved hands around the steering wheel and head out on circuit for the first time – it's all worth it! I remember that first race at Brands Hatch as though it was yesterday. That burst of excitement as I exited the pitlane and descended Paddock Bend for the first time, my first give-and-take battle with another car, that feeling of pure escapism and focus on the job in hand.

I completed five seasons and the thrill never waned. If you've done track days, then you'll have a vague sense of what racing is like – yet competition is on a different level. You enter a different zone where nothing matters other than extracting maximum performance from the car and getting past the car in front. In each race, you reach a pitch where you feel you can do no wrong and that you're free of consequence. It's a rare and precious experience in today's world.

I was never on the front of the grid simply because my budget car wasn't quick enough. Yet that never mattered: a battle for position is a battle for position no matter whether it's for pole or 17th.

Racing the Tiger is right up there with the best things I've ever done.

Adam Wilkins (*Complete Kit Car*)

Adam Wilkins with Dad, ready to race!

Chapter 12
GTA (Grand Tourer Avon) bodywork

Tiger has designed a new 'slippery shape' body as an alternative to the traditional roadster shape. The new design is, of course, available as a new model, but also as a retro fit (aftermarket conversion) for all other Avons built either by the factory or by the amateur at home.

The new Grand Tourer bodywork is designed to easily fit an existing Tiger Avon with only small additions to the chassis – the correct wheel offset will be required if the car is being assembled for submission to the ministry IVA test – plus a different roll bar or modification to the existing one.

You will need a small bracket/hinge assembly manufactured by Tiger to fit the bonnet, which will operate on the nylon bushes supplied. The front part of the central body (engine side) is pop-riveted to the existing alloy battery tray panel, with the interior sides of

Grand Tourer Avon.

the new central body pop-riveted to the existing top chassis rails on the Avon chassis. The lowest part – rear of the body section – has a steel plate riveted and bolted to the lower rearmost chassis member on the existing Avon chassis. The two sill panels for the GTA feature two small stays that bolt to the front of the chassis on both sides, and 6mm x 25mm bolts are used to join the lower flange of the central body to the upper flange of the sill panel. Lastly, a steel or wood spacer is bonded to the top chassis rail on the existing Avon, centrally between the top seatbelt anchorages and the underside of the body (just behind seat headrest).

The hinge/bracket fitted to the front of the existing Avon chassis (with the wheels fitted and front tracking completed). Centralise the body with the steering in the straight-ahead position and drill the chassis tubes with a 8mm bit and fit with 8mm bolts and locknuts – the hinge assembly is held on with 10mm bolts and lock nuts.

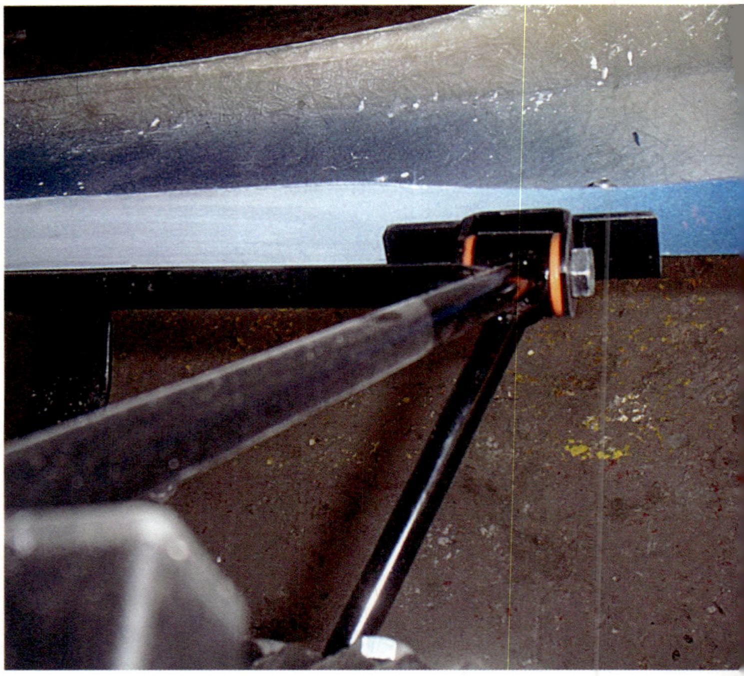

Above and top of following page: More views of hinge/bracket.

The sides of the GRP, where it reaches the existing top rail of the Avon chassis, are riveted with 12mm x 3.2mm rivets. The interior trim panel could be fitted at the same time.

The side panels riveted on another car.

The stays at the front of the sill panel: 8mm holes and 8mm bolts are used with locknuts. Before you drill the holes check for clearance of tyres on full lock.

The body and sill bolted together with 6mm bolts; the bolts are positioned approx every 150mm.

This shows the roll bar – there is a large normally square section spacer bonded under this flat area on rear of body.

The roll bar modification (or new one) has new seatbelt mounting points. The underside of the rear body section is bonded – with a spacer (wood or metal) – to the top rail on the chassis with a PU adhesive.

The front edge of the new body sitting across the chassis/battery area: this is riveted. Not shown on this car, but you could fabricate an inspection panel in the alloy for checking/working on the brake pedals.

Engine bay.

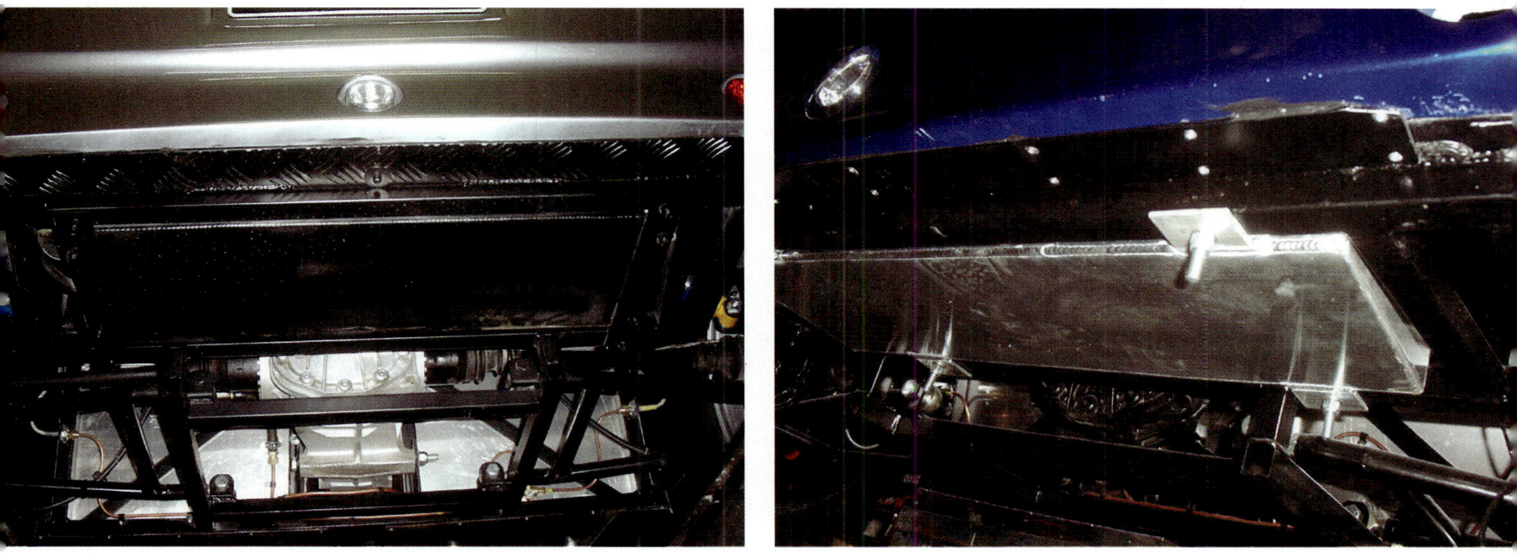

These pictures show the small plate that is drilled, riveted and bolted across the rear of the existing chassis and to the new underside of the body; the example on the left uses 5mm flat alloy plate, and the example on the right, 3.2mm flat steel plate.

Bonnet catch.

Sheet alloy is fabricated for better ducting of air through the radiator.

The bottom edge of sill panel riveted to the lower chassis rail. The exhaust side will have quite a large section of the GRP trimmed away for clearance of the silencer and to help with cooling. A flat steel bar (5mm x 25mm) is used to add support to the lower edge of the sill panel.

The dash and optional Aero screen (arrowed). The Aero screen is fitted with 3.2mm pop-rivets.

The head lamp cover is fitted by fabricating small alloy 90-degree brackets and holding with small self-tapping screws.

www.tigerracing.com
TIGER

Appendices

TIGER AVON SPECIFICATIONS

This section outlines the basic technical specifications of your Avon. At Tiger we run, as previously mentioned, our own Tiger race series (for most models of Tiger only). It's worth remembering that there is no substitute for a rolling road setup. In many cases at Tiger a rolling road session has outlined a problem with a component that could have failed during its next outing on circuit, and of course, knowing the bhp/torque figures of your engine and being able to monitor its performance is well worth while.

Rolling road setup.

These specifications are for guidance only and should be regarded as starting points. Individual cars should be setup to suit their owner's preferences.

Engine, gearbox & differential oil

Refer to the component manufacturer's recommendations. If racing your Tiger Avon you may want to use a higher specification engine oil.

Brake fluid

Refer to the donor vehicle manufacturer's specification. If racing your tiger Avon you may want to use a higher grade of brake fluid.

Wheels & tyres (tires)

Standard Avon bodywork will accommodate standard Sierra wheels (13, 14 or 15in) of up to 6J width and fitted with tyres of up to 195 section. If wider wheels are going to be fitted modifications to the standard bodywork will be required

Tyre pressures (road use)

Ford 'Pinto' SOHC-engined cars using 60 profile tyres:
Front: 22-24psi
Rear: 20-22psi
For cars with lighter engines, reduce these pressures by 2psi as a starting point.

Toe settings (road use)

Front track: total 4mm (2mm each side) toe-in.
Rear track: total 0-2mm(0-1mm each side) toe-out.

Camber (road use)

Zero. For racing see racing chapter.

Author's daughter Laura Dudley ready to race.

Castor (road use)

Usually 6 degrees works well, but may vary with different engines weights. For racing see the racing chapter.

Shock absorber (damper) settings (road use)

Front: usually 4-8 clicks (turning adjustment knob clockwise).
Rear: usually 3-6 clicks (turning adjustment knob clockwise).

Road springs

Front: these vary, but usual specification (for Ford 'Pinto' SOHC-engined cars) is 300lb (136kg) spring rate, 8in (203.2mm) length, inside diameter of 1 ⅞th inch (47.62mm).
Rear: these vary, but usual specification (for Ford 'Pinto' SOHC-engined cars) is 180lb (81.64kg) spring rate, 10in (254mm) length, inside diameter of 1 ⅞th inch (47.62mm).

Tiger has been using the above settings on Zetec cars and they usually work very well. For racing see the racing chapter.

Ride height

Between 114-127mm (4.5-5in) from underside of chassis to ground.

USEFUL ADDRESSES

Laura Dudley
Tiger Racing Membership (Racing dept)
Tiger Racing Limited
Unit 10
Anglia Way
Wisbech
Cambridgeshire PE13 2TY
Tel: 01945 466200 - 461423
www.tigerracing.com
laura@tigerracing.com
(For all tiger racing circuit enquiries)

BARC (British Automobile Racing Club)
South Eastern Centre
1 Tye View
Telscombe Cliffs BN10 7DN
Tel: 01273 588322
info@barc-se.co.uk

English Racing Automobiles
Tiger Racing Ltd
Unit 10
Anglia Way
Wisbech
Cambridgeshire PE13 2TY
Tel: 01945 466200 – 461423
jim@tigerracing.com
www.tigerracing.com
(Manufacturer of ERA racing and road cars)

Footman James (Insurance)
Waterfall Lane
Cradley Heath
West Midlands B64 6PU
England
Tel: 0121 561 4196

Motor Sports Association (MSA)
Motor Sports House
Riverside Park
Colnbrook SL3 OHG
England
(Racing licences)

Simon Ranson (technical diagrams)
Simon.ranson@ukgateway.net

Specialist Transport Advisory Utility Society (STATUS)
Department of Engineering & Technology
Manchester Metropolitan University
John Dalton Building
Chester Street
Manchester M1 5GD
England
Tel: 01625 873039
(Welding tests)

Tiger Owners' club
Adam and Richard Wilkins
57 London Road
Teynham
Sittingbourne
Kent ME9 9QW
England
Tel: 01795 521787
Tigtal@aol.com

First Principle Design Ltd
Pine Grove
Le Guet
Cobo
Castel
Guernsey GY5 7HH
Web: www.firstprincipledesign.com
E-Mail: simon.keys@firstprincipledesign.com
Tel: +44 (0)1481 259813

East Anglian Tiger Owners' club
www.eatoc.org.uk

Tiger Owners' club
www.tigerownersclub.co.uk

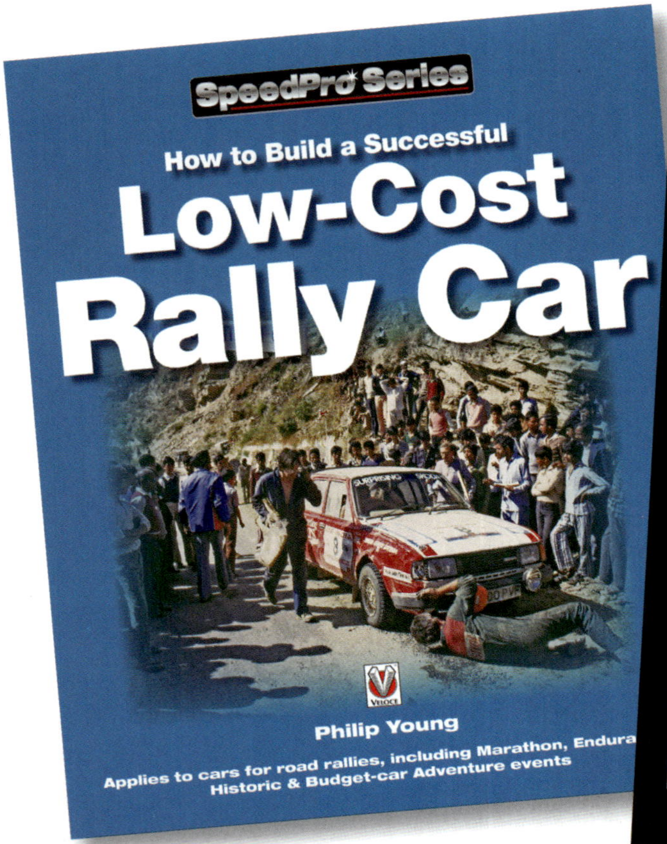
SpeedPro Series
How to Build a Successful
Low-Cost
Rally Car
Philip Young
Applies to cars for road rallies, including Marathon, Endura
Historic & Budget-car Adventure events

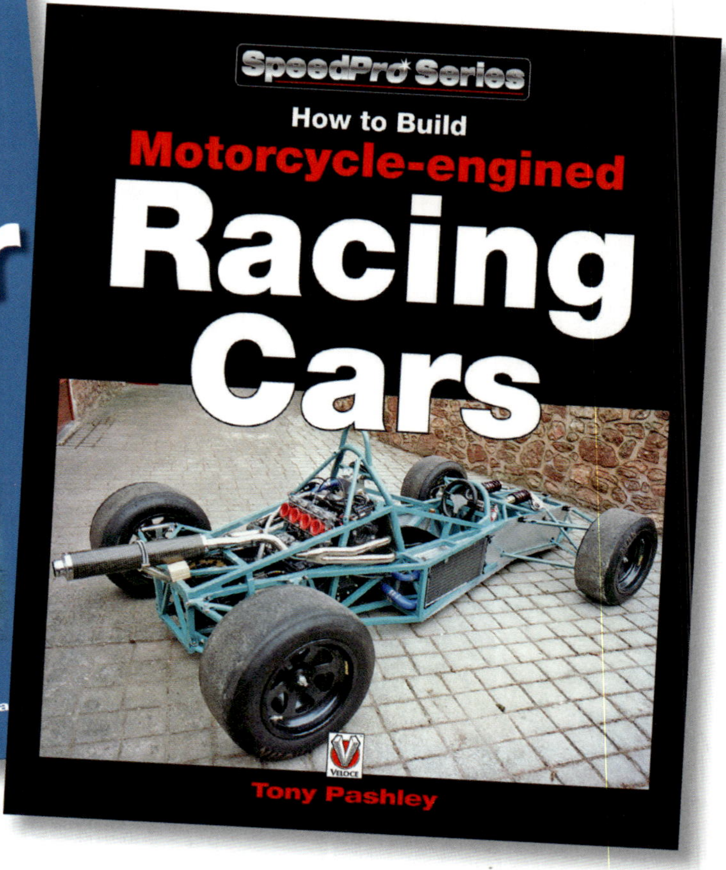
SpeedPro Series
How to Build
Motorcycle-engined
Racing
Cars
Tony Pashley

ALSO FROM VELOCE PUBLISHING

Build and tune your own high-performance engine.

Details the process of building four-stroke engines to a professional standard, from selecting materials and planning work, right through to methods of final assembly and testing. Written for the DIY engine builder in an easy-to-understand style, this is an essential purchase for all those seeking more power.

ISBN: 978-1-845842-97-0 • Paperback • 25x20.7cm • £19.99* UK/$39.95* USA • 128 pages • 201 colour and b&w pictures

Get the best handling and braking from sportscars/kitcars.

Get the best from sports cars/kit cars with wishbone front suspension, coil springs & telescopic shocks. Includes 'chassis' integrity, geometry, ride height, camber, castor, kpi, springs, shockers, testing & adjustment.

ISBN: 978-1-84584-207-9 • Paperback • 25x20.7cm • £19.99* UK/$39.95* USA • 128 pages

For more info on Veloce titles;
visit our website at www.veloce.co.uk • email: info@veloce.co.uk • Tel: +44(0)1305 260068
* prices subject to change, p&p extra

ALSO FROM VELOCE PUBLISHING

Build a reliable, high-performance 'Pinto' engine for road/track.

Build a reliable, high-performance 1600/1800/2000 'Pinto' engine for road/track, using many stock parts. Covers Cosworth versions of Pinto engines, too, and fitting Cosworth cylinder heads to Pinto blocks.

ISBN: 978-1-903706-78-7 • Paperback • 25x20.7cm • £19.99* UK/$39.95* USA • 144 pages

How to blueprint any 4-cylinder, four-stroke engine's short block for maximum performance and reliability.

Blueprint the short block of a 4-cylinder, four-stroke engine for maximum performance & reliability, without wasting money! Gives guidance on choosing bearings, crank, cylinder block, con-rods, pistons, camshaft, balancing, expert check-build procedures, and much more.

ISBN: 978-1-845844-14-1 • Paperback • 25x20.7cm • £17.99* UK/$32.95* USA • 112 pages • 195 colour pictures

For more info on Veloce titles;
visit our website at www.veloce.co.uk • email: info@veloce.co.uk • Tel: +44(0)1305 260068
* prices subject to change, p&p extra

Index